A Time and Times

A Time and Times

A Time and Times
My Memoirs

Dawn Voorheis Hawks

Publisher: Dawn Voorheis Hawks
Publisher Contact: dawnhawksbooks@gmail.com

ISBN-13: 978-1532746802
ISBN-10: 1532746806

Printed in the United States of America

Cover Design by: Brian Del Turco
Interior Design by: Bayside Graphics

Unless otherwise noted, Scripture quotations have been taken
from the New American Standard Bible (NASB), Copyright
© 1960, 1962, 1963, 1968, 1971, 1972, 1973, 1975, 1977, 1995 by The
Lockman Foundation.
Other Scripture quotations are Holy Bible, New International Ver-
sion®, NIV® Copyright ©1973, 1978, 1984, 2011 by Biblica, Inc.®
used by permission, all rights reserved worldwide; Holy Bible,
New Living Translation, copyright © 1996, 2004, 2015 by Tyndale
House Foundation, used by permission of Tyndale House Pub-
lishers Inc., Carol Stream, Illinois 60188, all rights reserved.

Dawn Voorheis Hawks

A Time and Times

Table of Contents

Grandchildren

Preface

Children's children are a crown to the aged.
Proverbs 17:6

"Grandma, you were born in 1937. Wasn't that during the Great Depression? Your parents must have told you about life when they were young. Did Great-grandpa fight in the war?"

"Wasn't your farm the first one settled in Bath Township? Didn't our Dutch ancestors come just forty years after the Pilgrims?"

"The Bath School disaster — all those children."

"Grandma, you're a living history! Have you ever thought about writing all this down? Would you do it for us?"

"Yes, I'll do it for you, Angela, and for all our grandchildren."

Has anything like this ever happened in your days
or in the days of your ancestors?
Tell it to your children,
and let your children tell it to their children,
and their children to the next generation.
Joel 1:2-3 (NIV)

I will teach you hidden lessons from our past —
stories we have heard and known,
stories our ancestors handed down to us.
We will not hide these truths from our children;
we will tell the next generation
about the glorious deeds of the LORD,
about his power and his mighty wonders.
Psalm 78:2-4 (NLT)

There is an appointed time for everything,
And there is a time for every event under heaven.
Ecclesiastes 3:1 (NASB)

Mom & Dad

Introduction

A couple of years before my parents passed away, my Aunt Jenny was in town visiting her daughter. This seemed a perfect opportunity to invite her, Aunt Edna, and Dad and Mom for an afternoon at our home.

They greeted one another warmly as old relatives and close friends do. They were soon chatting children, grandchildren, and great grandchildren, and health issues. A Bridge Club that had been meeting for more than fifty years, and mutual friends with whom they still kept in touch were among the topics that came up.

It wasn't long, however, until they drifted back to the decades when their lives had intertwined, beginning as young adults. I was surprised to hear Aunt Jenny remark, "You know, we lived in the best of times." Dad, Mom, and Aunt Edna agreed, and they began fondly reminiscing.

My parents and aunts were born at the turn of the century. Electricity and indoor plumbing were luxuries for most people until the 1920s. Automobiles were just becoming dependable and affordable. World War I had struck a severe blow to the nation, and the Great Depression and World War II were just around the corner. How could they conclude that those were the best of times?

The focus of my memoirs begins with the most impressionable period of my life, and I have chosen not to go beyond that point. Instead, I have written about the times and events which shaped my parents' generation — which they considered the best of times.

Through my research, writing, and my own observations, I came to understand why my elders viewed those years as the best of times. I see the American people pulling together with courage, duty, and honor for love of family, country, and God. They endured tremendous struggles and hardships and made untold sacrifices to preserve our way of life and build for the future. I saw the Greatest Generation.

I trust that you will enjoy reading this work and be the richer in understanding my Time and Times.

Dawn and work horses

Chapter One-
MY CHILDHOOD

"Daddy, look at the barn. It's so big! Do we have horses and cows?"

"Two work horses, Dawn. We'll get cows."

"What's that funny little building, Daddy?"

"That's the privy, Dawn. There's no bathroom in our house."

"Oh, Mommy, sometimes I have to get up in the night. It'll be dark. And when it's cold?"

"Honey, don't worry. We'll have a bathroom before we move."

"Well, Lil, let's go in."

"Carry me, Daddy. Jack, this is our new home!"

"I don't think your baby brother is going to remember this day."

• • •

The big, white farmhouse on the hill was cold and mostly empty. Dad set me on an old table in the living room near the front door, and some other people came and talked to Dad and Mom. It was March 1940. Little did I know then that I would live nearly sixty years on this farm near Bath, Michigan.

I would go to James Couzens Agricultural School, meet my future husband in eighth grade, and attend Michigan State University. I would marry, build a house on the farm, raise four children, and teach school. These years so full of precious memories would continue to be indelibly entwined with the lives of my parents.

• • •

Dad and Mom both grew up in the city. Although Dad's father was raised on the family farm, his grandparents had sold out and moved to the city by the time Dad was born. He only knew about farm life second hand and perhaps not always in the best light.

Future events would change that when Dad's paternal aunt and her husband moved from Lansing to a small farm about an hour away. Aunt Mable and Uncle Ed lived in the farmhouse and rented out the land. It was peaceful and quiet, far from the hustle and bustle of the city.

When Uncle Ed died, Aunt Mable was alone, and by that time in poor health. Since they had no children, Dad and Mom felt obligated to care for her, so they rented out our house in Lansing and moved in with Aunt Mable. Her handyman, Al West, lived nearby and continued to do outside chores and maintenance.

Following the move, life wasn't much different for Dad; he just drove farther to his job at General Motors-Fisher Body. But for Mom, it was quite different. Jack was a baby, and I was two. Aunt Mable was old and in poor health— and she was losing her mind. When she passed away a year later, Dad and Mom were comforted knowing that despite the challenges, they had given her their best possible love and care.

More than once Mom told me that our year with Aunt Mable was one of the most difficult of her life. But after moving back home, the city seemed so different. The city was smoking factories, bustling traffic, and constant noise. The country was quiet. It was fresh air, bright sunrises and brilliant sunsets over the hills, cattle grazing in green meadows, and waves of golden wheat. Dad and Mom had fallen in love with the country. That was the place to raise a family. Within a short time, they began looking for a farm.

"And we know that God causes all things to work together for good to those who love Him."

Romans 8:28

• • •

During the Depression, houses sold for pennies on the dollar, and Dad and Mom had pooled their savings to buy two modest houses in Lansing. They rented them out, and after they married, they moved into one of them. Later, the sale of both houses would provide the purchase price of a farm.

The search for a good farm within easy driving distance

Our family soon after we moved in

to Lansing paid off. The eighty-seven acre Hollister farm, on the southeast corner of Clark and Chandler Roads in Bath Township, was the answer to their dream. The acreage was right, and the soil was fertile. It was ten miles to Dad's job at Fisher Body, and two miles to the tiny village of Bath.

Al West, Aunt Mable's handyman, agreed to come as our hired man. He was tall, gray, and kindly. He didn't talk about a family, which was common for a man his age. The Great Depression had brought many good men to their knees.

Although the house had three upstairs bedrooms, my large walk-in closet was changed into a bedroom for Jack, leaving the third bedroom for Al. He lived in our house and ate at our table. He didn't have any teeth and often asked Mom for some "sody" for his frequent indigestion.

Our farmhouse

For a few years we became Al's family. Dad and Mom may have been the adult children and Jack and I the grandchildren Al never had, or lost during those ten terrible years. I often wonder how my parents could go from the city to cows and crops. Al worked alongside them, teaching and guiding in his quiet, unassuming manner.

• • •

For a while, Dad and Al farmed the old-fashioned way, with a team of tall, gray work horses. Dad came in for dinner one summer afternoon and announced that he had sold the horses.

I couldn't believe it. "But how can we pull the plow and the wagon?"

Dad smiled. "Dawn, you just wait and see!" The next day a flat-bed truck pulled up in front of the barn and unloaded a used Farmall 10-20.

"What are those funny things sticking out of the wheels, Dad? It bumps on the ground and makes funny tracks."

"Those steel lugs will work just fine. When the war is over, we'll get rubber tires." And that's just what we did.

Our first tractor — with lugs

The tractor was so much faster and easier than the horses. We didn't have to feed it or clean up after it. Gasoline was rationed, but because producing crops was part of the war effort, we had a farm gas ration card.

The Farmall M came out in 1949, and those fire-red tractors were our choice. Over the years we bought two, and we always scoffed at the "chug, chug" of the neighbors' noisy, green John Deere tractors.

• • •

Our house was on the east end of our Clark Road frontage, and the next farmhouse toward Bath was on the west end of the Armstrong farm. Our side yards were only about a quarter mile apart, separated by our small field and the Armstrong apple orchard.

As soon as we got settled, Dad and Mom wanted to meet our neighbor, Bill Armstrong. It was an easy walk to "Old Bill's." In the spring this path was lined with giant boughs of pink and white apple blossoms and in the fall with brilliant red and golden-yellow fruit.

Bill seemed to appreciate our strolling over. He enjoyed the company, and he liked to show us some of his wonderful things. Dad was particularly interested in his Civil War musket and tales passed down from that era. Mom loved the old-fashioned furniture and the pump organ in the parlor. Jack and I didn't care much about these, but we were fascinated by his gentle sheep, especially the lambs. Al just liked to visit with Bill and share stories of the joys and struggles of their often lonely lives.

Farming followed the main thread of those conversations. Farming was all Bill knew. He had grown up on this family farm and worked with and taken care of his parents until their deaths. Tragedy struck when Bill's young wife became ill and died. It wasn't very long after her death that their son died in his early twenties.

Bill had been alone now for many years. He was stooped and suffered from edema which progressively made him unable to work his farm. Dad and Al put up his hay and helped care for his sheep. We also began renting Bill's land and planting more crops.

Al and Bill's friendship grew during those years. As Bill's health continued to decline, Al offered to move in with him.

Al took care of Bill until he died when I was about eight — and then Al left us. Maybe he felt he could no longer keep up with the rigors of farm work. Maybe he needed to try and find another friend, another life.

Bill's will read that his farm was to remain in his family, and two nieces living in Grand Rapids were his only heirs. These women had never been part of Bill's life and had no interest in his property. With the help of a lawyer, the will was "broken" so that we could proceed with the purchase.

A drainage ditch — which we called the creek — had just been cut through the Armstrong land. At the final closing on the land, Dad brought up the subject of the five-hundred-dollar ditch tax that would soon come due, and the nieces agreed to pay it.

However, after the final papers were signed, Dad mentioned the tax again. One of the nieces flatly stated, "We never put that in writing, and we aren't going to pay it." Dad and Mom were from the old school where a person's name is only as good as his word. They were deeply hurt — and not only financially.

• • •

After the purchase of the Armstrong farm, we now owned one hundred seventy-four acres. Since there was now a second farmhouse, we could take on a hired man with a family. Over the years we had several: some good and a few that didn't last more than a week.

Since we had to have a steady source of reliable labor

Dad and Mom in the back yard

during the busy summer months, Mom decided she could pitch in with the outdoor work. My petite mother, at five foot two inches and one hundred pounds, learned to drive the tractor. She could plow a straight furrow and cultivate corn without digging up a single stalk. And she could pull the hay wagon without jerking. The teenage boys hired from the community during haying season really appreciated my mother. They didn't have to worry about being thrown backwards and sideways while stacking fifty-pound bales five feet high.

Mom never complained about doing field work, but sometimes she and Dad would disagree about how something should be handled. If Mom felt very strongly about it, she had a plan. She would walk across the road and discuss it with our neighbor, Lloyd Rosekrans. If he agreed with her, he would have a conversation with Dad, as farmers do, about the dry spell, whether the corn would be knee-high by the fourth of July, if the wheat crop would go forty bushels an acre. Dad or Lloyd would eventually get around to Mom's concerns — without mentioning her, of course. Dad would later tell Mom what amazing insights Lloyd Rosekrans had.

Sometimes Dad would quit the shop for a while. When times were hard or major purchases of farm equipment were necessary, he would go back, and Fisher Body was always ready to rehire him. During the war years, automotive manufacturing turned to aircraft production. Although he was too old to serve in the military, Dad contributed to the war effort both in the factory and on the farm.

• • •

My growing-up years seemed to be divided into two parts: school days when farm and city life probably weren't much different, and the long, glorious three months of summer. Summer was the farm.

My kindergarten photo

We didn't have any neighbor children so my playmates became my cats and kittens.

Grandma Voorheis often remarked, "Dawn, you are going be an old maid and live with twenty-five cats."

My love of cats began when I was in kindergarten. I rode the school bus with a teenage girl named Betty Boutwell. I was little with long, blonde curls Mom carefully wrapped around her finger each morning. Betty told me I was cute, and I was pleased that this grownup girl would talk to me.

One afternoon near the end of the school year, Betty asked me an amazing question. Would I like a yellow, striped cat named Butterball and her kitten? I was so excited that I couldn't wait to get off the bus and tell Dad and Mom. Of course, we went to the Boutwell farm that evening.

Butterball was beautiful, and she seemed to like me. She purred and rubbed her soft, golden fur against my legs. But her kitten was different; it was scrawny and couldn't stand up. Betty explained that she wanted to find a new home for Butterball and her kitten because a neighbor's male cat had killed the other three kittens.

I was so excited to take my treasures home. As we made a bed in the barn, Dad and Al took stock of the situation. They agreed that the kitten had been too badly hurt to live. They didn't want me to watch it die or find it dead.

The next day when I got home, I ran to the barn. Butterball was waiting for me, but where was her kitten? Dad and Al

Snooks and me

explained that the kitten had died. As Dad wiped away my tears, he promised that next spring Butterball would have more kittens. And she did. She had four adorable little balls of fluff, and my favorite was a yellow-striped male I named Snooks.

Spending time with the kittens was a highlight of my summer. I loved to hold and snuggle them, and it was so much fun watching them play and chase one another. But late in the fall, they seemed to play less and less — and they stopped eating.

"Dad, look at these kittens. They aren't eating; they must be sick." Dad had noticed too, and we tried to get them to drink warm milk. We put them next to Butterball, and she licked them affectionately. Then in desperation, Dad and I held them and tried spooning milk into their mouths. But nothing worked. Snooks and the other three kittens died, and I was heartbroken. Dad and I carried them out beside the barn and buried them. I picked a wild flower and put it on Snooks' grave.

Butterball usually had her kittens up in the haymow. She would look fat and then disappear. It was fun to play detective and sneak around waiting for her to come out to eat. I'd very quietly follow her up the ladder and find the very spot where her soft, furry, hay-scented babies were nestled.

In the spring Butterball had another four kittens, and one was a yellow-striped male. I had another chance. I named this baby after my first Snooks and loved him just as much. We couldn't believe it when the same scenario played out that fall. We buried this Snooks next to my first one.

Dad decided that this couldn't be a coincidence. When Doc Zeeb came to check on our cows, Dad questioned him about our kittens. It was most likely enteritis, germs of some sort in the soil, and there was a medicine we could try.

We went to Don's Drugs in Lansing where Dad bought his cow supplies. The druggist carried the medicine for the kittens, and I was hopeful. But when he said it was three dollars, I was stunned. How could it cost so much? Money for cows was a necessity, but for cats? It still brings me to tears when I remember how much my dad loved me and cared about what was important to me.

Butterball had four kittens again that spring, and I had my third Snooks. Surely the medicine would work, and this time I'd have this cat for many years.

In the fall when the kittens stopped eating, we followed the druggist's instructions and forced the medicine into their mouths. But Snooks got sicker and sicker. This wasn't supposed to be happening; he should be eating and playing again. But to no avail, and my cat cemetery continued to grow.

Surprisingly though, Mitsy and Kitsy, two calico females, started eating again. For some unknown reason the medicine had saved them. Then, like a miracle, the kittens they later had seemed to have immunity, and our cat population soared. At one time we had twenty-three, all living in the barn, catching mice, and drinking the warm milk Dad poured into their basin at milking time.

Butterball died, so I never had another Snooks. But the following spring, my favorite of Mitsy's litter was a little gray, fluffy kitten named Toby. He was one of those kittens that would go limp when I held him. I could turn him over and hold him in the crook of my arm like a baby doll. I loved him as much as any my three Snooks.

Jack and me on the turkey range

For a few years we raised turkeys to supplement our income from milk and grain. The poults were kept in brooder houses until they were big enough to be put out on the range. When they were close to market size, people would park on Chandler Road, sneak across the field, and steal them. At night we usually kept three German shepherds tied on the outskirts of the flock to bark and growl in hopes of scaring off the thieves.

Early one summer, we needed another guard dog so we went to old Homer Petters' farm on our back road. He raised German shepherds, and we had gotten pups from him before. The only dog he had for sale was an ill-tempered, mostly-grown dog he called Wolf. Dad had no choice but to buy him. He put a dog coop at the east corner of the barn and chained him there. Jack and I were afraid of this dog, and Dad warned us to stay away from him.

One day when we were working in a field close to the road, we found an older kitten that had apparently been dropped off. It was half-starved, and we took it home.

We were horrified the next morning when we saw Wolf tossing the kitten up in the air and violently shaking it to death. I had never seen anything like this before, and I was even more terrified of that dog.

Dad warned me, "Dawn, now we know that Wolf kills cats, but we need him this fall. Your cats follow you so when you go behind the barn; always go around on the west side."

One morning Jack and I went out to the pond behind

the barnyard to shoot frogs with our BB guns. I don't know how I could have forgotten Dad's warning so quickly, but we walked on the east side of the barn, keeping a safe distance from Wolf.

Dad was working, and Mom was plowing in the field beyond the pond. Grandma Voorheis had come for a short visit and was in the house. After a little while I could hear her calling, "Dawn, Dawn!" I couldn't imagine what she wanted, but I reluctantly walked back toward the house. Grandma was on the back porch pointing.

"Dawn, that dog's got your cat." And there was Toby, my precious kitten, being violently tossed around like a rag doll. I threw down my gun and ran back through the barnyard, past the pond to the field. Mom stopped the tractor in anguish at what I was about to tell her.

"Mom, Mom, that dog's got Toby. He's shaking him; he's killing him! Oh, Mom, it's my fault. I walked past Wolf. Oh, I wish I were dead! I wish I were dead!"

Mom pulled me hard into her arms. "Dawn, Dawn, don't ever say that! Don't ever say that!"

We ran to the barn, and Mom got Toby away from that dog. She told me to get a box from the granary, and I prayed all the way, "Lord, please don't let Toby die. Please!" But of course, every bone in his little body was broken. Mom gently laid him on a soft towel in the box. She gathered me in her arms, and my mother cried with me.

The next morning, I found my BB gun lying in the wet dew. I picked it up, carefully dried it off, and put it away. Dad had taught us always to take good care of our things.

• • •

During the warmer months, the cows were put out to pasture. Lady, our black and white English shepherd, was our herder. We'd point and say, "Lady, go get the cows." She would bolt away toward the pasture with Jack and me running after her. After she circled and rounded them up, the cows would walk in single file back to the barnyard.

Dairy cattle must have a two-month dry period before calving, so we usually had about twenty-five producers at any one time. Besides grass, each cow received some grain as determined by her stage of gestation. It was my summer job during evening milking to put just the right amount in each cow's manger. Dad always made me feel needed, an important part of our team, and I never wanted to disappoint him.

• • •

When July rolled around, it was time for combining wheat and oats. This was a huge job and seemed to take a very long time. Dad would pull the combine around the field while Jack and I stayed on the wagon—sometimes parked under a tree, but usually not. When the bin was full, Dad would pull up next to the wagon and lower the chute.

Jack and I would hold a burlap bag, and one of us would yell, "Ready!" Dad would start the grain flow, and when the bag was full, we'd tie up its mouth with binder twine. Early on, the bags were too heavy for us, so Dad would move them to the back of the wagon. This process got faster once Jack and I were old enough to drive the tractor and pull up beside Dad wherever he was in the field.

Combining was hot, itchy work. Sweat would run down our faces, and dust and chaff would cling to our skin and clothes. We raised a lot of grain, and harvesting seemed to go on and on. Sometimes I felt guilty wishing for a rainy day when I could curl up in the house with a good book. But wheat and oats were needed for cattle feed and seed for planting, and the remainder brought a good price at the Bath elevator.

26

• • •

During the 1940s, although war was on the other side of the ocean far away from us, there was an even greater threat to America's children, especially in the cities. From 1944 to 1955, the United States experienced ten severe polio epidemics, with an outbreak in 1952 being the worst in our nation's history. The majority of children contracting polio had only flu-like symptoms and fully recovered. In the more serious cases, the outcome varied from mild weakness of an arm or leg to complete paralysis—and even death, if muscles controlling breathing or the brain were affected.

It was obvious that the disease was contagious, but no one seemed to know how it was transmitted. Outbreaks mainly occurred during the summer months. Dad and Mom never took us to the beach, and we didn't go to movies or any other crowded gatherings. Some cities closed theaters, public swimming pools, and sports areas. Children were warned not to drink from public water fountains.

When I was in the ninth grade, Janet Densteadt moved to Bath, and we became good friends. She walked with a slight limp, and one day I asked if she had hurt her leg. She said she'd had polio when she was two, and the muscles in her left leg were weakened. That foot was two shoe sizes smaller than the other, and it seemed strange when she always had to buy two pairs of shoes.

One summer when I was in my early teens, I didn't feel good, and my neck was stiff. Mom panicked. Our family doctor was retired, but my mother's gynecologist could see me that Friday afternoon. After examining me, he said it could be nothing or any number of things, but a spinal tap was the only way to rule out polio.

We went to a nearby clinic, and I was taken into an examining room. A doctor came in and began trying to get a

March of Dimes poster

long needle into my spine. The nurse held me as I cried in pain. An "angel" doctor suddenly appeared on the scene. He told me to do sit-ups, and I put all my might into it. After a moment he patted me gently on the shoulder and announced, "This young lady doesn't have polio!" Mom breathed a huge sigh of relief, and I made a life-altering decision.

Young women in my day who wanted to continue their education basically had two career choices—nursing and teaching. My girlfriend, Shirley Robson, and I had decided at an early age to be nurses together. We'd go through the St. Lawrence Hospital nurses' training program and become registered nurses. Growing up, I just knew I'd make a good nurse. After all, I took care of sick cats and watched my dad vaccinate cows and pull calves.

After the attempted spinal tap, my back was so painful that I could hardly move. I lay still for a couple of days and mulled things over. I didn't know where my anger was directed—at my poor, panicked mother; at her doctor with little, if any, experience with polio but with an open appointment; at the doctor with the needle; or at the disease itself which brought so much fear and dread into our lives. But then and there I decided that I wanted nothing to do with the medical profession.

We know that God allows circumstances into our lives to teach and direct us. I'm so thankful that I didn't have polio. I'm also thankful that He allowed me to go through that frightening experience so that He could reveal His plan for me. Shirley would go on to get her white cap and pin; I would get my teaching certificate.

Shortly before I graduated from high school, polio was considered conquered. Over a two-year period, nearly two million second- and third-grade children participated in field trials conducted by the Poliomyelitis Vaccine Evaluation Center at the University of Michigan.

On April 12, 1955, it was announced to the world that the Salk vaccine was up to ninety-percent effective in preventing paralytic polio. It became available in 1957, and the Sabin vaccine was licensed in 1962. Future generations would no longer have to live in fear for the lives and health of their children.

• • •

While summer was the farm, kittens, and time in the barn with Dad, winter was school, friends, and time in the house with Mom.

Michigan winters can be brutal, and severe storms have a devastating effect, especially in rural areas. The Great Blizzard of 1947 started on the east coast and rapidly swept westward. Heavy snowfalls knocked out power lines and completely isolated us from the outside world.

No power meant no heat because the stoker that fed our coal-burning furnace was electric. In order to stay warm, we lived in the kitchen and closed off the rest of the house. The bottled gas stove gave off some heat and melted snow for drinking. We had produce and canned goods in the basement.

Even in a blizzard, cows have to be milked twice a day. With no electricity to run the milking machine and the cooler, Dad had to milk by hand and dump out the milk.

Jack got sick, and we feared it was pneumonia, but there was no possible way for Dr. Martin to come from DeWitt. Jack lay on the daybed covered with blankets and Mom hovering over him.

Finally, a group of Bath men decided that the only way out was to dig out. Armed with shovels and pulling a sled loaded with sandwiches and thermoses, they began clearing the five-mile stretch down Clark Road to U.S. 27.

The Great Blizzard of 1947

Jack Wiswasser, owner of the local garage, rigged up some sort of snow plow on the front of his tow truck. As they "liberated" a farmhouse, the grateful family brought out food and hot coffee.

With Clark Road open, Dr. Martin could come. Jack did have pneumonia, but he quickly recovered, thanks to penicillin, which had only recently been mass-produced for the military.

Usually children are happy for a snow day, but not in this case. We didn't have school for two weeks.

• • •

Wash day was a major event. Mom would fill the wringer washer with hot, soapy water. After the agitator sloshed the clothes around, she'd put them through the wringer and into the rinse tub. After another time through the wringer, they were ready to hang on the clothesline.

In the summer our clothes and sheets would dry quickly and smell like the fresh outdoors. In the winter, however, they would freeze. Sheets were stiff, white sails blowing in the breeze, and jeans were half-men or boys strangely standing up by themselves. To remedy this, Mom would turn our living and dining rooms into tent city, stretching clothesline hither and yon. We'd use several collapsible wooden-peg racks near the floor registers for smaller articles.

• • •

Just as Dad had the radio on in the barn, so Mom had hers on in the kitchen. She listened to soap operas: *Young Doctor Malone*, *The Romance of Helen Trent*, and *One Man's Family*.

Jack and I didn't pay much attention to the programs Dad and Mom listened to, but every weekday evening at seven-thirty, we were glued to the radio."Hi-yo, Silver! Away!" The Lone Ranger, the masked man, rode his white stallion with Tonto, his faithful Indian companion, at his side. They conquered evil, lived justly, and served as role models to generations of children.

On Saturday mornings at eleven o'clock, we couldn't wait to hear the next children's classic on *Let's Pretend*. As Rapunzel, I could let down my long, golden hair so the handsome prince could climb up and save me. I could ride in an elegant carriage with Cinderella or watch in awe as the frightful, repulsive green frog turned into a marvelous, majestic prince.

On Sunday afternoons we shivered with gleeful anticipation while Lamont Cranston fought crime as an invisible avenger. "Who knows what evil lurks in the hearts of men? The Shadow knows!"

While Jack and I were getting ready for school, we listened to grandfatherly Happy Hank who would try to sell us on the delectable flavor of Coco Wheats—"the creamy, hot cereal with the cocoa treat."

Sometimes it was difficult to separate the fiction of radio shows from reality. One morning Johnny McGonigal came into our third-grade classroom and said incredulously, "Happy Hank knows me!"

We all gasped. "But how?"

"I don't know how, but he does! He said, 'Johnny, don't come to the breakfast table without combing your hair.' How did he know I forgot? How does Happy Hank know me?"

• • •

Books were a major pastime year round. Mom was a member of the Doubleday One Dollar Book Club, and every month, her carefully-chosen book arrived in our mail box.

Mom loved to read to us as well. Jack and I would sit on each side of her in the living room and hear the most fascinating stories. When Black Beauty's friend Ginger died, I cried. When Bambi's mother was killed, I cried. Mom would gently say, "Dawn, I know it's sad, but I can't keep reading with you crying."

I'd sniff, and Mom would snuggle me a little closer and wipe away my tears.

As Jack and I got older, we checked out many wonderful books from our school library. Books took us to far away, fascinating places where we experienced the life and times of famous and ordinary people alike, going with them through the struggles, sorrows, and sweet times of their lives.

• • •

Occasionally, we would go to a Sunday afternoon movie in Lansing. I was seven or eight when we saw *Arsenic and Old Lace*. When Cary Grant popped up outside a window overlooking the window seat hiding the body of one of his aunts' "charity cases," Jack and I nearly jumped out of our seats.

About a year later, we saw *Our Vines Have Tender Grapes*. When the neighbor's barn was burning, I cried with Margaret O'Brien as her father helped the farmer frantically lead his

Our family out on a Sunday afternoon

prize cattle out of the flaming timbers. And I cried harder at the sounds of gun shots directed at those cows they couldn't get out.

When I first heard about television, I imagined actors standing in front of their microphones reading scripts. I was soon corrected. "But no," people said, "we'll see it acted out."

Like in the movies? I couldn't believe it!

We got our first television when I was fourteen. We set it against a wall in the dining room and put chairs in front of it like at the movies. It was only a fourteen-inch screen, so we sat pretty close and turned off the lights. The screen was often snowy, and we'd wrap aluminum foil around the rabbit ears and twist them this way and that to try and get a clearer picture.

There were only a few shows we'd watch or could watch, so we didn't spend much time in front of the television. However, I no longer had to use my imagination. I could actually see the Lone Ranger and Tonto riding off into the sunset.

• • •

For the vast majority of children, the family farm is a thing of the past. Some grandparents tell about it, and some write about it. I'm so thankful that I have had the privilege and blessing of doing both.

As I look back, farm life was hard, and it was uncertain. We had to be concerned about the weather all during the growing season. Ill-timed rains could turn partially-cured rich, green alfalfa hay into bleached, yellow stalks. Drought could rob us of an abundant corn harvest; high winds could flatten wheat, the tops heavy with golden grain. Grown turkeys could be stolen, and cows could get mastitis.

Jack and I learned to work hard at an early age, and our life on the farm *was* work, but so much more. It was what we did. A family—a team—working our soil, bringing in our harvest, caring for our livestock, and taking in the beauty of God's nature. And for me, it was also breathing in the fragrant hay-scent of soft, furry baby kittens.

Dawn Voorheis Hawks

Mom in her early twenties

Chapter Two-
MY MOM

"Lillie, get up! Get up off that grave. He's gone; he's gone. Oh, Lillie, you're so young. You've got to go on with your life."

"I know, Mother Taft, I know."

• • •

One rainy afternoon, Jack and I were lying on the living room rug playing a board game. Mom had been quiet that morning, and it wasn't like her.

"Jack, do you think Mom's sick? She was really quiet when we were eating lunch."

"Oh, Dawn, you worry too much. You know how hot it was yesterday, and she was out helping Dad most of the day. She's just tired."

"I hope you're right. Your turn, Jack."

A few minutes later, Mom came into the living room. "Children, stop your game for a few minutes. I want to talk to you." She sat down on the davenport. "Come sit here beside me."

Mom seemed very serious. I just knew it. She was sick—
or something even worse.

"Mom, what's wrong?"

"Oh, nothing to worry about. I've had something to tell
you both for a long time, and I think you're old enough now
to understand. I haven't said much about my growing up
years and my life before I met your dad."

She paused and took our hands. "Something very sad
happened to me when I was young. I was married for only a
short time, and my husband was killed in an accident. That's
when I came to Lansing. I don't like to talk about it, but I
wanted you to know. It was a long, long time ago."

Avoiding our eyes, Mom went back to the kitchen. I didn't
say anything or ask anything; I understood then that the subject was closed.

"Jack, we should never ask Mom any questions about
this."

"Okay, but I told you she wasn't sick. Come on, Dawn.
It's your turn."

When we were in our late teens, I mentioned something
about Mom's previous marriage. Jack was surprised—he
hadn't even remembered. I remembered, though, and as I got
older, I began wondering more and more about this man my
mother had loved and married.

• • •

After Mom's stepfather died, we went up to my Grandma
Agler's house in Edmore. We stayed for a few days after the
funeral so that Mom could help Grandma tie up loose ends.

"Lillie, what am I going to do with Charlie's clothes? I
don't think any of the boys would want them. What did you
do with Howard's clothes?"

Howard—this was the first time I had ever heard his name.

I knew Mom kept in contact with a woman named Mrs. Taft. They exchanged Christmas cards and infrequently talked on the phone. Mom never mentioned who Mrs. Taft was, and I didn't ask.

Mom had a cedar chest in her large walk-in closet. Looking for something one day, I raised the top and discovered some astonishing things: an album with most of the photographs torn from its black pages—and letters from a man named Howard Taft. Even though I felt guilty, my curiosity got the best of me. I began reading. These were love letters from the distant past, and it was obvious that this man loved my mother very much.

There were two faded newspaper articles. One stated that Howard Taft had been severely injured in the construction of the Second National Bank building in downtown Saginaw. He was doing masonry work close to the elevator shaft.

According to the article, the alarm on the elevator at the construction site had yet to be installed, so there was no warning when the elevator descended. It was assumed that Mr. Taft leaned back to view his work just before he was hit. His face was crushed, and he had severe head injuries. The doctors thought he might make it, but the second article stated that he died the next morning. He was twenty-two.

Where was Mom when she heard the unspeakable news? Was anyone with her through that long night vigil? Did Howard regain consciousness? Did he speak? Could he speak? Did Mom bargain with God? Would she become embittered towards God? She kept all the answers buried in the recesses of her shattered heart. She and Howard had been married fewer than three months.

Howard Taft

• • •

Many years later, after I had married and was raising a family of my own, our daughter Lisa and my brother's daughter Terri were playing at my parent's house one afternoon. The girls went upstairs with Mom to put away the laundry. Bored and curious, they started rummaging in one of Mom's dresser drawers. Lisa picked up a photograph of a man standing in front of a car. "Who's this, Grandma?"

Mom seemed surprised, but she wasn't annoyed. "Oh, I thought I'd gotten rid of all those. His name was Howard Taft. He was my first husband — and he was killed."

"He's handsome, Grandma."

And Mom replied thoughtfully, "He was every bit as good as he was handsome."

• • •

That time of courtship and marriage was the happiest Mom had ever known up to that point in her life. She later confided to a close family friend of her heartache and despair following Howard's death. She had never believed that a man like Howard Taft could love her, and Mom had experienced little love.

Her years growing up were very tense and demanding.

Mom's half-brother Don's wife once remarked that my grand-mother was a "difficult" woman. Her first marriage to Mom's father, Ira Outman, didn't last long. She soon married again, had a son who died in infancy, and divorced a second time.

When Mom was five, Grandma married Charlie Agler and bore seven more children. Unfortunately, Mom didn't seem to belong—she wasn't part of Charlie's brood. She was punished while Charlie's children "got away with murder." She couldn't participate in sports or other activities after school because she had to "get home and help."

Seemingly, Mom's main haven of solace during those difficult years was in the home of her mother's sister, Aunt Blanche, and Blanche's husband, Uncle Henry. Their daughter Vernice was six years younger than Mom.

Mom about five years old

Mom would go to her aunt's house when her half-brothers got into boy-hood mischief, and Char-lie "went on a yelling ram-page." The Gray house was peace while the Agler house was pandemonium.

One morning in her early teens, Mom woke up horri-fied—she thought she was ill or dying. Rushing to the Gray's, Aunt Blanche consoled and hugged her. "Lillie, hasn't your mother ever told you? This is just a part of becoming a young woman."

• • •

I don't know what Charlie did to make a living. He built the sun porch on our farmhouse, so he must have been skilled at carpentry and could do odd jobs. He wasn't lazy or irresponsible, but he had many mouths to feed. Sometimes beans and coffee were all they had for days, and at one point, they lived in a woodshed.

• • •

The Agler family moved from Edmore to Owosso for a brief time. Mom walked to elementary school past the home of James Oliver Curwood. She had no way of knowing then that this man would become one of America's most popular wilderness-adventure writers. Many of his novels would become movies, and his future home, Curwood Castle, a popular tourist attraction. Mom only knew that he was a kindly man who paused in his front yard to talk to a lonely, young girl.

Mom was enchanted by the narratives of Mr. Curwood's travels to the far north and the novels he had written. She couldn't believe it when this great man autographed and gave her some of his books. Unfortunately, when she moved out of the Agler home, she didn't take them with her.

Later, when she went back for them, they were gone. Maybe they were discarded as worthless. Maybe they were given away or sold for pennies. But I like to think that in someone's library, a copy of *The Danger Trail*, or *The Flower of the North*, or *Kazan, the Wolf Dog*, signed and inscribed "To Lillie," is treasured.

• • •

Perry and Jay Outman, her father's younger brothers, attended Edmore High School with Mom. Perhaps their pleasant conversations emboldened Mom to try and connect with her father. One day, she went to the Outman farm, and Mrs. Outman kindly directed her towards the field where her husband was working. Mom didn't have to introduce herself.

"You're Lillie. You look like your mother."

Ira Outman seemed pleased to see Mom, but he gently explained that he couldn't enter into a relationship with her. Memories of my "difficult" grandmother may have played a role. Could Mom have expected this response or was it another page of rejection in her unfortunate book of life?

• • •

In the fall of Mom's senior year, the Grays moved to Saginaw. Mom deeply missed them, especially Aunt Blanche. As soon as Mom graduated, the Grays welcomed her into their home, and she soon found a job. It was in Saginaw that she met Howard Taft.

• • •

After Howard's death, Mom needed a place to start over — a place to get away from her merciless memories. One of her high school girlfriends, Myrtle Dryer, had moved with her parents from Edmore to Lansing, and they invited Mom to board with them.

Mom got a job as a waitress, and one day the boss made a pass at her. She threw down her apron, disgustedly exclaimed, "I quit," and walked out.

She then enrolled at Lansing Business University and took stenography courses. Before graduation she was offered a job in the office at Oldsmobile, and although she regretted failing to graduate, she just couldn't pass up this opportunity.

My mother was an attractive young woman, and sometimes she was asked to pose for advertisements. In one pho-

Mom modeled for Oldsmobile

tograph she is at the wheel of the first Oldsmobile convertible. Fifty years later when the last Delta 88 convertible rolled off the assembly line, this photo appeared with the lead story on the front page of the Lansing State Journal.

• • •

Despite her difficult upbringing, Mom seemed to harbor no resentment towards her mother and stepfather. We would drive up to Edmore every so often, and Grandma and Grandpa would come to the farm on occasion.

Every Christmas, Grandma would send a box with small gifts for the family. Jack and I always received children's classics.

In later years, Grandma changed so much. I choose to remember her as she was then, going to the small bookstore in Edmore and selecting a special book that perhaps she had loved as a child—this one for Dawn and that one for Jack.

Two of Mom's half-brothers, Jim and Don, moved to Lansing after they married. We visited them a few times, but Mom never felt close to them.

After Charlie's sudden death, their son Bill moved in with Grandma. As the years went by, she became increasingly agitated and uncontrollable. I'll never forget the last time I saw her. She frightened me when she grabbed my hand and said, "Dawn, they're trying to get me." Her face was twisted up — more like anger than fear.

"Who, Grandma?" but she went on raving. Finally, her children had no choice but to commit her to the Traverse City State Hospital for the insane where she died.

• • •

On a warm summer afternoon when I was sixteen, I was busy with some outside chores. Mom and Dad were working, and Jack was at a friend's. As I strolled from the barn to the house, I noticed an old car pulling into our driveway.

I walked up, and the elderly driver rolled down the window and asked, "Is this the Voorheis farm?" He seemed relieved when I nodded "yes."

As he helped a small, aged woman out of the car, he explained, "I called your mother's brother to get the directions here. He told me Lillie has two children." Almost apologetically, he went on. "You must be Dawn. Probably your mother didn't tell you about me. I'm her father, Ira Outman. This is my wife, Nellie."

Mrs. Outman smiled. "We're so pleased to meet you, my dear. We hope it's all right for us to drop in on you like this. We don't mean to be no trouble, but my husband so wanted to see Lillie and meet her family — while's there's time. Is she home?"

"No, Mom's still at work," I hastened to add, "but she'll

be home soon. Please come in and sit down. Let me get you a glass of cold water."

While we visited, I kept wondering how I was going to introduce this man to my mother. Was I going to say, "Mom, I want you to meet your father"?

I was relieved when Mom drove in just a few minutes later. In spite of the years, she recognized her father from that lone visit so long before. She didn't hesitate; she stretched out her hand, and Grandpa Outman grasped it tenderly in both of his.

"I wanted to see you, Lillie. I hope you don't mind us just coming like this." With tears streaming down her face, Mom assured him that she was overjoyed.

"I want you to meet my wife, Nellie." Mrs. Outman smiled and extended her hand. Mom gently took it in warm welcome.

"Lillie, we've brung some little gifts. They ain't much though, but we wanted to give you something so's you'll remember us."

How could we ever forget this gracious, humble man — Mom's father, my grandfather — and his precious wife? This visit was to linger in the years to come as a cherished memory for all of us, but especially for Mom.

Grandpa and Grandma Outman accepted the invitation to stay for supper and spend the night. They talked with Mom all evening. Did Ira Outman explain why he couldn't have been a father to her? Could he have done anything differently? Did Mom understand? Was there anything to forgive?

Whatever transpired during those brief hours brought reconciliation — and heartfelt affection — between Mom and her father. Grandpa Outman died a few years later. On that warm summer evening, his presence, his caring brought closure to his daughter in his humble way — the only way he knew.

• • •

After retirement, my parents sold the land and later the house and outbuildings. When they were getting ready to move, I helped Mom pack up the house. Walking past her bedroom one afternoon, I saw her taking old letters and photographs out of her cedar chest. She looked sad but resolved as she started down the stairs.

As smoke from our burning barrel drifted up on the soft summer breeze, I didn't ask Mom what was in flames — but I knew.

Dad's new automobile

Chapter Three-
MY DAD

"Ada's got another boy. She named him Arthur George."
Thus penned my grandmother's older sister Angeline in her
diary on November 3, 1905.

• • •

Dad was born into a middle-class family, the second son
of Fremont and Ada Tarte Voorheis. Uncle Ed was two years
older, and Aunt Min completed the family five years later.

Both of my grandparents came from large families. Grandpa was the seventh of eight children born over a twenty-three-
year period to John and Mary Voorheis. Before Grandpa and
his younger brother Arthur reached adulthood, their siblings
had left one by one to set out on their own paths.

With advancing age and fewer sons to work the land, my
great grandparents sold the family farm and moved to the
city of Saginaw. Tragically, Arthur was diagnosed with con-
sumption (tuberculosis) and passed away in his twenties. Out
of esteem for his brother, Grandpa named my father Arthur
George.

• • •

Grandma Voorheis was the youngest of ten children born to Louis and Mary Tarte, French Canadian Catholics, who immigrated to Western Michigan in the late 1800s. They lived in Bay City where her father worked as a ship's carpenter.

When Jack and I were very young, we went to a Tarte family reunion. There were numerous relatives there—aunts, uncles, and cousins.

Dad took us over to a white-haired couple seated together on a bench in the backyard. "Pape and Mamen, I want you to meet my children, Dawn and Jack." They didn't speak much English, but we knew that they understood when they nodded, smiled, and clasped our hands. It was the only time I ever saw my great-grandparents.

As her only living granddaughter, some of Grandma's effects were passed down to me after her death at age ninety-six: a set of crystal goblets, a cut glass sugar and creamer, many photos, Angeline's diary—and a faded letter from my grandfather dated February 3, 1902.

In 1902, both of my grandparents were still living at home, Grandma in Bay City and Grandpa in Saginaw, a distance of fifteen miles. The letter began with some casual news about his job and his parents. Grandpa was pleased that they would soon move into a more modern house with running water.

Then, Fremont Voorheis began expressing hurt and indignation. Since it was his understanding that he and Ada were courting, why had he heard that she had "been seen with another fella?" After a few more pointed questions and comments, Grandpa's tone seemed to soften; he thought "things were going to work out."

What did he mean? Could these startling words be a prelude to a marriage proposal? Was he beginning to soften his stance on the obstacles inherent in their religious differences? Both sets of parents had been voicing strong objections to this budding relationship, fearing that it would lead to courtship — and a mixed marriage.

In the early twentieth century, the mere thought of a Catholic marrying outside the faith was virtually unknown. The Church made such rigorous demands on the non-Catholic that unless he or she had no or few religious convictions, submission was virtually intolerable.

The relationship continued to flourish. Courting began in earnest, and Grandpa proposed.

After declaring an intention to marry, the Church required a course of instruction in the obligations placed on the non-Catholic. The children must be baptized by a priest and instructed solely in that faith. The Catholic must begin in earnest to try to convert the marriage partner.

It's unlikely that until these conditions were disclosed, Grandpa fully comprehended the course ahead, not only for himself, but for his children. He quickly stated his strong objections. He would no longer continue the course of instruction nor agree to the terms laid down by the Church.

This declaration sent the Tarte household into a frenzy of anguish and dread. Would Ada marry outside the faith? The decision was now fully in her corner — to reject the basic tenants of the Catholic Church or marry Fremont Voorheis?

Months followed with much soul searching, and finally the decision was made. Fremont Voorheis and Ada Tarte were married by a justice of the peace.

For a time, Grandma seemed willing to relinquish her religious ties. However, with the birth of their first son, her resolution faltered. Since Catholic tradition holds that baptism removes original sin, an unbaptized baby's death results in an eternity in limbo. Fearing for her children's souls, Grandma arranged for each of her three children to be baptized secretly.

The Voorheis family never attended any church, and the

Dad's family (Dad on the right)

children were given the option of going to a neighborhood Sunday school or of not going at all. Over the course of his childhood, Dad sporadically attended several.

Billy Sunday, national league baseball player turned evangelist, held a revival at South Baptist Church in Lansing when Dad was ten. One evening, Mr. Sunday asked for a couple of boys to assist him with an illustration, and Dad volunteered. He always felt honored to say that he had been on the platform with the greatest American evangelist of the early twentieth century.

When Dad was in his mid-fifties, he began attending church with Mom, Jack, and me. More than forty years after that chance meeting, he accepted Billy Sunday's message of repentance and faith in Jesus Christ.

• • •

When Dad was growing up, the Fredericks family lived across the street. They had several children, and their daughter Edna was about Dad's age.

Chuck Emmett lived around the corner, and Dad, his brother Ed, and the Emmett boy were best buddies on into adult life. They walked to school together, played baseball, went fishing and swimming in the Grand River, and hung out as boys do.

The neighborhood friendship that began in childhood blossomed into dating and romance in high school, and Chuck Emmett and Edna Fredericks eventually married. They never had children, and we claimed them as our Uncle Chuck and Aunt Edna. Holidays always included them; they were an integral part of our family. When I was sprinkled at age six months in the First Methodist Church of Lansing, they accepted the responsibility of being my godparents.

• • •

I only remember meeting Mr. Fredericks once when he lived for a brief time with the Emmetts. He was in his nineties, and he reminisced about my dad as a boy. Dad was in his sixties at the time, and I couldn't believe that someone still living could have known my dad when he was young.

• • •

I was always curious about Dad's childhood, and Aunt Edna was a wealth of information. After all, she was the girl across the street.

In later years, I was visiting Aunt Edna one day, and of course, the subject turned to the Voorheis family. After chatting about them for a few minutes, she related, "Mr. Voorheis was a good father, and he spent a lot of time with his children, especially his boys. They had big celebrations of birthdays and Christmases and Independence Days. He was always taking pictures, even of ordinary events like his boys playing baseball. We saw lots of pictures over the years, and he was so proud he could develop them himself."

Aunt Edna's face clouded. "But your grandfather wasn't a good husband." She stopped short, apparently rethinking what she had just related. "But that's all in the past." And she went on recalling pleasant memories of growing up with Art and Ed and Charlie. But I never forgot what she said, and it seemed that I would never know what she meant.

• • •

After Dad's stroke at age eighty-seven, there was concern about his peripheral vision loss which would put an end to his driving. Dad and I sat in the office waiting

Grandpa Voorheis and children skating on the Grand River

for the ophthalmologist. I don't recall what prompted our conversation to drift in this direction, but he said, "Dawn, I was never unfaithful to your mother." As an afterthought, he added, "And it wasn't that I didn't have the chance. There were all kinds of women at the shop. One might give a guy 'the eye,' and say, 'How 'bout going out for coffee or a drink after work?'"

"No, I was never unfaithful. But my dad wasn't faithful to my mother." Struggling for control, he went on. "One evening at supper, Ed, Min, and I were talking about our day at school. I mentioned something about our spelling bee and a girl in my class, Margaret Crowden.

"Dad hadn't been paying much attention, but when he heard that name, he got all flustered. 'Who did you say? Margaret Crowden? Why are you talking about her?' I couldn't imagine why he was so upset.

"It was our spelling bee, Dad. She spelled science with 'ei' and I spelled it right.'"

My dad's face clouded, and he was ten years old again. "One morning, my mother said, 'Arthur, your dad forgot his lunch. You can catch him if you hurry.' I picked up his lunch bucket and ran down the street. And then I saw him—standing on the corner with Mrs. Crowden."

He paused and went on. "But he made it up to my mother when he got sick. She took care of him until he died."

The doctor came in, and our conversation ended. I was left with many questions, and I can only speculate how my grandfather might have "made it up to" his wife.

As Fremont Voorheis slowly wasted away, his stomach eaten by cancer, Grandma was called upon to be more than a wife. She assumed the roles of nurse and caregiver. For many months my grandfather lay in bed suffering long, painful days and longer nights—so much time for reflection.

When I was in my teens, Dad gave me a small Bible belonging to his father. Hebrews 8:12 is marked: *Jesus Christ the same, yesterday, today, and forever*

I choose to believe that as death drew near, my grandfather remembered his former roots. John Wesley preached repenting, confessing sin, and asking forgiveness, not only from God, but from those one had wronged. I can only hope that my grandparents had in their last days what they must have had in their first days of young love.

• • •

I don't remember my grandmother ever talking much about her earlier life, but hardships and difficulties didn't seem to make her bitter. Like his mother, Dad pretty much took the curves of life the way they were pitched to him.

Dad was a good student. He wanted to attend college and study architecture, but it was not to be. With Uncle Ed married and starting his own family, Dad felt responsible to support his mother and sister. Peddling papers and doing odd jobs didn't bring in much. At the end of each semester, Dad would go to the employment office at Fisher Body.

"How old are you, son?"

"I'm eighteen, sir." Dad's boyish appearance always gave him away.

"Eighteen? Come on back in a couple years." Dad would complete another semester of high school and try again.

When he was seventeen, he was finally offered a job on Fisher Body's auto assembly line. Every pay period, he handed his paycheck to his mother. Even though he didn't finish high school, he saw that his sister did.

Uncle Chuck had a supervisory position in the sewing department at Fisher Body, and he offered Grandma a job. The majority of his employees were women, and even his own mother worked for him.

Grandma was only forty-five when she was widowed, but she never sought outside employment. Who can say what her reasons were? Who can say if it was fair?

One of Dad's greatest regrets was not being able to graduate from high school. He didn't blame anyone — it just made him sad.

• • •

Watching his father suffer a slow, agonizing death at age forty-nine affected Dad more than we might have imagined. In his late forties, he began experiencing stomach pains. He wouldn't use the word *cancer*, so he told Mom he might have an ulcer.

I don't remember much about the "soft diet," but I do remember milk toast—poached eggs on toast, swimming in warm milk. I couldn't imagine eating it, but Dad didn't seem to mind. Even though changing his diet didn't help, Dad still resisted seeing a doctor.

To me "ulcer" was a strange and frightening word. What if my dad were really sick? What if he should die like Grandpa Voorheis?

My fear grew, especially when I couldn't help overhearing Mom and Dad talking. "Lil, I'll be all right. Let's just wait a little longer to see if the diet helps."

"Arthur,"—Mom only used his given name when she was serious—"you can't wait any longer. I'm so worried. We've just got to get to the bottom of this." So Dad finally gave in.

Relief and elation were the only words to describe what we all felt when the report came back. There was no stomach cancer, not even an ulcer—just worry and stress. Dad gave up his milk toast and never mentioned his stomach again.

• • •

Dad was a man of character and integrity. Those qualities, which enabled him to sacrifice for his mother and sister, carried over into his care for Mom, Jack, and me.

I loved my dad. I loved being with him, working with him, learning from him. Sometimes when I asked a question, Dad would go into more detail than I actually wanted. He was a natural teacher, and I'm so thankful that I inherited that gift.

On more than one occasion, Dad related, "When your mother was expecting Jack, people would say to me, 'You must be hoping for a boy this time.' Oh, that would be nice I'd say, but I really wouldn't mind having another one just

Dad and Dawn

like Dawn.'"

It has been said that children acquire their view of God from their fathers, either for good or ill. My father made it easy for me to believe in a God of love. As a little girl, when I walked alongside him on a smooth or stony path and needed the security of his touch, I'd place my tiny hand around his little finger—and I was safe.

And along both the smooth and stony paths of my life, God's strong, secure "little finger" has been there, His Almighty Hand reaching out to me in unspeakable love.

Dawn Voorheis Hawks

Dad and Mom on their wedding day, September 1, 1934

Chapter Four –
THE GREAT DEPRESSION

"Lil, let's get married!"

"Married? But, Art, we can't. I'll lose my job. You know Mr. Reuter thinks married women shouldn't hold a job when so many men can't find one."

"I know what A.J. says, Lil, but he won't let you go. He couldn't get along without you. But if it makes you feel any better, we'll keep it quiet for a while.

"Ed and Jenny are leaving for Chicago next Saturday morning, and we can go with them. You remember Norm and Sylvia got married in a Methodist minister's home just across the state line. And there's no waiting period in Indiana.

"How many couples can say they honeymooned at the Chicago World's Fair – even if it's only for a weekend?"

So Dad and Mom were married on September 1, 1934, during the height of the Great Depression. They were both twenty-nine.

• • •

The Roaring Twenties were a time of great prosperity. With the advancement of technology and increase in the number of large corporations, the economy was thriving, and the market was booming. Rising stock prices reflected not only good times, but the expectation that those good times would continue.

People were making more money, and easy credit enticed some to speculate on the market by plunging into debt. Billions of dollars were invested in anticipation of great returns. So many people followed this trend that stocks became inflated—selling for more than they were worth.

During early October 1929, the buying craze began to wane, and on Thursday, October 24, the bottom fell out. Stock prices plummeted and continued to fall as investors tried to unload their holdings. At the end of the day, the New York Stock Exchange had lost four billion dollars.

By the following Monday, people began to comprehend the dire situation. Panic ensued. Stocks were virtually worthless. On October 29—the day known as Black Tuesday—throngs rushed to the banks to draw out their savings, and the banks began to fail. The Great Depression had begun.

• • •

Cities attracted beaten people from all parts of the country. Foreclosures forced farm families to pack up and move to the cities. City dwellers, unable to pay their rent or mortgages, were evicted into the world of public assistance. Charities, missions, and churches opened soup kitchens and helped multitudes.

At the peak of the Depression, seventeen thousand families were put out on the streets each month. By 1932, twelve million Americans were unemployed, and approximately one out of every four breadwinners no longer had an income.

Depression era soup line

Families rose to the occasion and made sacrifices. Crowded multi-family houses and apartments were common. Sometimes beds were used in shifts as night workers slept during the day, and day workers at night.

Millions of Americans were desperate. Out of work and with dependent families, men bore the brunt of the despair, feeling ashamed and humiliated.

• • •

The bottom soon fell out of the auto industry. Not unexpectedly, Dad lost his job when Fisher Body closed.

Plato once said, "Necessity is the mother of invention." Dad couldn't invent a job, but he could adopt a new perspective on what he might do or learn to do. Although not yet married, he still had his mother and sister to support, so he began looking for any kind of work he could find.

Dad heard about a position at a small dairy store in the village of Williamston, about fifteen miles east of Lansing. With his optimism and enthusiasm, Dad took over its management, and he learned by listening, observing, and doing. He made cheese, cottage cheese, and butter. He turned the residue of the butter-churning into buttermilk.

Dad bought from local farmers and sold a quart of milk for twenty-eight cents and a dozen eggs for fifteen cents. He enjoyed visiting with his suppliers and customers and listening to their tales of hard times. He offered words of encouragement, and now and then, added a little extra for a family in desperate straits.

• • •

Dancing was a popular form of recreation during the Roaring Twenties. Dance parties were carefree — the gaiety of the youth-centered lifestyle celebrating good times. The happy-go-lucky mood of the twenties came to an abrupt halt with the crash.

Entertainment in some form was necessary to cope with life's challenges, and with hard times, people had to be creative. Without lavish dining and drinking, dancing became low-cost entertainment.

The Pine Lake Dancehall, a short drive from Lansing, was a popular spot to spend a weekend evening. It wasn't uncommon for young men and women to "go stag" — attend without a dance partner. In fact, dances were a great place to "meet someone."

One particular Saturday evening, Myrtle and some other girlfriends talked Mom into going to Pine Lake. Uncle Chuck and Aunt Edna coaxed Dad into joining them.

After a while, Uncle Chuck nodded over his shoulder. "Art, see that good-looking girl over there? Why don't you ask her to dance?" Dad shrugged, but he went in her direction. After the song ended, Uncle Chuck asked, "Well, Art, how was it?"

"She's a swell dancer, but she seems kind of quiet and reserved."

Myrtle and the other girls also were curious. "He sure is

good-looking, and he seems so polite and gentlemanly. What do you think, Lillie?"

"He's very nice, but he just wanted someone to dance with."

Myrtle wondered aloud. "I don't know, Lillie. I wouldn't be surprised if he came around again." Mom was surprised when he did.

At Pine Lake with their friends, Dad and Mom would bump into one other and spend most of the evening dancing. It didn't take much encouragement from Uncle Chuck and Aunt Edna for the two couples to begin double-dating.

Dad and Mom were just casual friends for the next couple of years. And then they began to spend more and more time together. They played golf on weekends or early mornings before work. Mom attended Dad's city league baseball games and cheered him on.

There were good times with Uncle Chuck and Aunt Edna: dancing, catching a movie, or playing bridge.

They also enjoyed family times with Grandma, Aunt Min, and Uncle Ed and Aunt Jenny. The family all loved Mom, but they wondered how this friendship could become more than just that. Grandma must have wondered, too.

As time went on, Dad and Mom began to confide in one another. Dad told her about his father's death and his family obligations. She was fascinated by his industry and ingenuity in operating the dairy store. Mom felt safe with him. He listened and seemed to understand. She could share her unhappy childhood—and her devastating loss.

But both of them had misgivings. Although Dad clearly liked this young woman, he was by no means in a financial position to begin a serious relationship. And Mom was still grieving. This was to be a lengthy relationship due to the complexity of their lives and the circumstances of the times.

Dad and Mom finally courting

• • •

After completing her stenography course at Lansing Business University, Aunt Min was offered a position in the office at Oldsmobile. She and Dad continued to live at home, and she was now able to contribute to their mother's support.

Aunt Min began dating Al Seyfried, and they wanted to get married. In order for both her and Dad to get on with their lives, they had to make some kind of arrangement for their mother to be self-supporting.

Because the family home was rather large, it was feasible to transform it into three apartments — one on each floor. The first two floors would be rentals, and Grandma would live in the attic apartment. The remodeling began in earnest.

The renters were carefully chosen. They generally became friends with Grandma and helped look after her. The house was close to the bus line, and with the rent money, she became quite independent.

Aunt Min married, and Dad moved with his mother into the attic apartment. He was now able to put away additional funds.

• • •

On March 4, 1933, during the height of the Great Depression, Franklin Roosevelt delivered his first inaugural address with the memorable statement: "Let me assert my firm belief that the only thing we have to fear is fear itself." He promised to act swiftly to face the "dark realities of the moment." These words gave the American people confidence that their newly-elected president would take bold steps to solve the nation's problems.

Five days later, Congress passed the Emergency Banking Act which reorganized the banks and closed the ones that were insolvent. In his first "fireside chat," the president urged people to put their savings back in the banks, and within weeks, almost three-quarters of the nation's banks had reopened.

Numerous public projects were set in place to provide jobs and boost public morale. The WPA — the Work Progress Administration — put some eight and a half million people to work on constructions projects such as roads, bridges, parks, airports, and public buildings.

The NYA — the National Youth Administration — was a branch of the WPA. It provided work and education for young people between the ages of sixteen and twenty-five.

The CCC — Civilian Conservation Corps — was under the control of the U.S. Army. President Roosevelt believed that this civilian "tree" army would relieve the rural unemployed and keep youth "off the city street corners."

Focusing on soil conservation and reforestation, millions of trees were planted on land made barren by fires, natural erosion, and lumbering. Corpsmen dug canals and ditches, built wildlife shelters, stocked rivers and lakes with nearly a billion fish, and cleared beaches and campgrounds.

In the first two years, over five hundred thousand youth had lived in CCC camps, most staying from six months to a year. Nearly three million participated over the course of the program.

The army's experience in managing such large numbers and the paramilitary discipline required of corpsmen provided an unexpected preparation for the massive call-up of civilians brought on by the ensuing war in Europe.

• • •

In 1933, Fisher Body established a satellite plant on a portion of Lansing's vast Oldsmobile factory grounds. The expansion boosted output to fifteen hundred cars a day, making the Olds Motor Works the fourth largest in the automotive industry. At least four thousand new employees were hired, and Dad was one of the fortunate.

Civilian Conservation Corps poster

Mom was working for the Reuter Brokerage Firm, and she and Dad both had good jobs for the times. Houses sold for nickels on the dollar, and they pooled their resources to purchase two small houses in Lansing. The rent money contributed to their savings.

• • •

Eight years after that chance meeting at Pine Lake, circumstances were finally favorable for Dad and Mom to marry. They moved into one of the houses, the bungalow on Miller Road, where I was born two and a half years later. Jack completed our family when I was two. Except for a year in Nashville, we lived on Miller Road until 1940 when we bought the farm.

Even though it was difficult, Dad and Mom agreed that waiting to marry was the only reasonable decision for the times. And Dad was right. After three months of dread, Mom finally gathered the courage to reveal her secret. "Mr. Reuter, I just have to tell you. Art and I got married."

Dismayed, he managed to ask, "Oh, Lillian, you aren't going to quit, are you?"

A typical Dutch combined house and barn in the 1600's

Chapter Five-
MY DUTCH HERITAGE

"Dad, what nationality are we?"

"Well, Voorheis is a Dutch name. My dad told me that some of our family came over from Holland six generations ago."

"Six generations? But six generations from whom? Your dad? Your grandfather?"

"I don't know, Dawn. That's all he told me."

• • •

Drenthe was the least populated of the northeastern Dutch provinces. The low, often wet land was unfavorable for producing good crops. A long depression, beginning in 1650, was particularly problematic for tenant farmers, triggering rising taxes, high rent, and low grain prices. Hard times became a justification for land owners to allow houses, barns, and outbuildings to fall into disrepair.

The prospects awaiting those who dared venture to the New World were becoming even more enticing.

71

• • •

The colony of New Netherland was established by the Dutch West India Company in 1624. A successful Dutch settlement grew up on the southern tip of Manhattan Island and was christened New Amsterdam. Freedom of religion and free trade were instituted from the beginning.

A few residents began buying large tracts of fertile farmland on western Long Island in 1636. As the population continued to grow, magistrates and militia officers were elected, and in 1654, the village of Amersfoort was officially named.

In 1651, about a hundred people left Drenthe to undertake the long voyage to New Netherland. Gerri Jacobs and Jan Stryker were among them. These two families chose to settle in Amersfoort, and in a brief time, they became prominent members of the community.

• • •

Steven Coerte was born in 1600 on a farm in the little hamlet of Hees. His first wife died in 1643, leaving him with three children, and his second marriage, six years later, added five more.

Steven had worked on at least three different farms. For men like him, owning his own land was a powerful motivation for change.

Another compelling incentive was personal information about life in Amersfoort. Mrs. Stryker and Steven's second wife were sisters.

After much soul searching the decision was finally reached. Nine years after the Strykers left, Steven was ready to follow. He was sixty years old and had six small children.

Departing from Amsterdam on April 15, 1660, the family sailed aboard the *De Bontge Koe — the Spotted Cow*. Captain Pieter Lucasz was the ship's master. Little is known about the

The small farming hamlet of Hees

ship itself, but based on similar ships of the times, it was probably about one hundred seventy feet long and fifty feet wide.

Besides Steven and his wife, the family consisted of an adult son and daughter from Steven's former marriage: Coerte Stevense, and Hendrickje and her husband, Jan Kiers, and three sons and three daughters from Steven's second marriage. These children ranged in age from ten to a baby born sometime during the year of the voyage.

There were nineteen people from southwest Drenthe in New Netherland before the *Spotted Cow* brought thirty-nine more. By 1664, there were one hundred eight, the majority on Long Island.

That year, New Amsterdam was captured by the British, and the city was renamed New York in honor of the Duke of York. Ten years later, all of New Netherland was under British control, and the colony became New York State. To foster a successful transition, the British allowed Dutch landholdings to remain. The Hudson River Valley preserved its traditional Dutch character until the early nineteenth century.

• • •

Under British rule, Steven Coerte adopted the surname

Van Voorhees—"from and before the village of Hees." He is the patriarch of the Van Voorhees family in America, and everyone with any variation of the name is his descendant.

• • •

Opportunities offered in the New World were not exaggerated. After leasing only fourteen acres in Hees, Steven became a large landowner in Amersfoort. Seven months after his arrival, he bought a house, brewery, and thirty morgens (sixty-three acres) of land for three thousand four hundred guilders. After sixteen years, his holdings had almost doubled.

In addition to managing his farm, Steven served as magistrate in 1664 and administrator of taxes in 1683. The Coertes were founding members of the Amersfoort Dutch Reformed Church.

After a full, rewarding life in the New World, Steven died at age eighty-four, bequeathing his estate to his five surviving children.

There is a street named for him in Sheepshead Bay, Brooklyn, and a commemorative marker reads:

> *Steven Coerten, born 1600, migrated with*
> *his family in 1660 from the manor Voor-hees,*
> *Province of Drenthe, the Netherlands, to the*
> *village of Amersfoort, now Flatbush, Long*
> *Island, and settled near this site. He served his*
> *church as deacon and elder, and the communi-*
> *ty as a magistrate and patentee in the Nicills*
> *Charter of 1667.*

Traces of Dutch influence such as homes, family surnames, and the names of roads and whole towns remain in present-day southeastern New York State and northern New Jersey.

• • •

Coert Stevense Van Voorhees, the eldest son of Steven Coerte, was twenty-two when he arrived in Amersfoort. He married and became a deacon in the Dutch Reformed Church. At age twenty-six, Coert served as a representative in the assembly held at City Hall. Twenty-five years later, he was captain of the militia, and his land holdings had exceeded those of his father.

Cornelis Coert Van Voorhees, born in 1678, was the seventh of nine children born to Coert Stevense. He was baptized at the Amersfoort Dutch Reformed Church and married in 1700. In that same year, he began serving as an ensign in the militia.

Coert Van Voorhees, born circa 1701 at Amersfoort, was the eldest of five children born to Cornelis Coert. He was a trustee of the Presbyterian Church in Cranbury, New Jersey, in 1739. He owned a house and forty-two acres on Carnarsie Lane in Brooklyn. Built before 1641, this house is the oldest standing in that area. Coert died circa 1775 in Middlesex County, New Jersey.

John Voorhies, born in 1729, was the eldest son of six children born to Coert. He married circa 1750 in Somerset County, New Jersey. He died in 1800 and was buried at Bedminster Cemetery, Somerset.

John Voorhees, born in 1753, was the second of John's four children. He married in 1773. His wife died childless, and he remarried in 1787. Nine children were born to this union. The family moved back and forth between Albany, New York, and the state of New Jersey.

Joseph Voorheis, born in 1793, was the fourth child of

John. He was baptized in the Dutch Reformed Church, Albany County, New York. His wife died ten years after the birth of their fourth son, Charles. As part of the great western expansion, Joseph moved his family to Michigan sometime before 1840, and he owned property in Oakland County. Charles, a private in Company A Twenty-Two of the Michigan Infantry, was killed in action on January 4, 1863, in Lexington, Kentucky. He was buried in Oakland County.

John E. Voorheis, born in 1835, was the second of five children born to Joseph. He married Mary Jennings in 1858, and they had eight children. John E. died in 1900 and was buried in Forest Lawn Cemetery, Saginaw, Michigan.

My grandfather, Fremont J. Voorheis, born in 1876, was the seventh of eight children born to John E. He was our ninth generation of Dutch immigrants. Dad, born in 1905, was the tenth, making me the eleventh.

My grandfather told Dad some six generations before had come from the Netherlands. My original question was: "But six generations from whom?"

The mystery is solved. The sixth generation was John E. Voorhees, born in 1753, my grandfather's great-great-grandfather.

I'm so thankful that my grandfather passed on what he knew, and that Dad handed it on to me. Otherwise, I would have missed out on tracing my genealogy in America back to 1660, just forty years after the Pilgrims landed.

• • •

The Van Voorhees Family Association recently joined Facebook. I came across a posting about DNA testing of direct male descendants of *Steven Coerte*. I began researching and found some amazing information. DNA shows the paternal lineage as Haplogroup J2a1b, consistent with Semite people.

This haplogroup is not standard Northern European found among Dutch Doggerlanders.

• • •

Israel as a nation ceased to exist in 70 A.D. when Roman Legions, led by Titus, crushed a four-year revolt, sacked Jerusalem, and destroyed the temple. Thousands were murdered, but some escaped and scattered throughout the Roman Empire. Many sought refuge in Spain.

In the late fourteenth century, Spanish Jewry was threatened by mobs of fanatical followers of the Roman Catholic Church. Thousands were tortured and put to death, and it is estimated that more than one hundred thousand saved themselves by converting.

By the mid-fifteenth century, those who had been baptized into the Catholic Church but continued to practice Judaism in secret—*Marranos*, meaning *pigs* in Spanish—formed a compact society.

Jews began to grow rich in business and rise to high positions in the state and the royal court. They intermarried with the noblest families. Jealousy, hatred, and suspicion arose, charging some with being untrue to the Catholic faith. The fury spread until it was directed against all Jews.

In March 1473, riots broke out with bloodshed and looting. Fanatical mobs carried out massacres from city to city. In 1480, the Spanish Inquisition was introduced to provide institutional control over the persecution of Jews. In the first year, more than three hundred were burned, with their estates going to the Crown. The number of victims grew into tens of thousands.

In 1492, the Edict of Expulsion ordered all Jews out of Spain. Many fled across the border into Portugal, but they were forced out five years later. Since the Netherlands belonged to Spain, it was natural for Spanish Jews to emigrate there. Although some maintained their Jewish religion and culture, by the mid-1600s, many forced converts had rejected Catholicism and become members of the Niederdeutsche, later the Dutch Reformed Church.

• • •

I am a direct descendant of Steven Coerte. In writing my time and times, have I stumbled on a part of my genealogy leading back to Father Abraham?

Dawn Voorheis Hawks

Main street of Bath in 1955

Chapter Six-
THE CUSHMANS

"Oh, I love black cherries. My pail's almost full. Mom, why did they plant all these cherry trees here in this field? And what about those lilac bushes over there beside the road?"

"Dawn, we asked the same question when we were buying this farm. Mr. Hollister explained that this hill was the Cushman Cemetery."

"Cemetery? But there aren't any gravestones."

"The bodies were dug up and moved down to the Gunnisonville Cemetery, but they couldn't find them all. Mr. Hollister guessed that's why these trees were planted — so this hill couldn't be worked."

"Mom, the Cushmans must have lived here a long time ago."

"More than a hundred years. They were the first settlers on this land."

"Mom, who were the Cushmans?"

• • •

I am connected by blood to the life and times of Steven Coerte, who came to America from Drenthe, the Netherlands. I am connected by land to the life and times of Ira and Belinda Cushman, who came to America from Kent, England.

• • •

Our farm, on the southeast corner of Clark and Chandler Roads in Bath Township, was originally called the Cushman farm. Growing up, there were many Cushmans in the Bath area.

Josephine Cushman Vail, mother of one of my classmates, Betty Vail, once remarked, "You can't walk down Main Street without running into a Cushman."

Bird and Agnes Cushman owned the farm to the west across Chandler Road. Dad liked to tell of our first meeting with the family. Mr. and Mrs. Cushman and the girls, Elaine and Alta Jean, had come over one afternoon to meet us. As Dad reached out to shake Mr. Cushman's hand, he remarked, "Bird, you've got two swell granddaughters."

Bird smiled and replied, "Art, these are my girls. I just got started a little late." We loved the Cushman girls, and they became our babysitters.

Bird's older sister, Lucy Cushman Morrison, lived down Clark Road across from her brother. I enjoyed visiting her and hearing tales of her youth and of relatives and peers I only knew as older citizens of the Bath community.

I once mentioned that Bird's house was small and didn't look like other farmhouses. Mrs. Morrison showed me a photo of their childhood home, a large two-story farmhouse, and sadly remarked that it had burned to the ground.

She recounted tales of attending the Cushman School on the corner across from our farm. For a time, the school house

Cushman School

was also used for church services. A new pastor was coming one Sunday morning, and the custodian wanted to make a good impression. He built a roaring fire in the pot-belly stove, and regrettably, it overheated, burning down the school house. Fires were all too common in those days.

Who were the Cushmans? When did they come? Why did they come?

Researching the family line, I learned that their roots trace back to Robert Cushman, who was instrumental in the Mayflower crossing and establishment of the Plymouth Colony.

• • •

In 1611, due to religious persecution by the Church of England, a group of Pilgrims left Kent seeking religious freedom in Leyden, Holland. Robert Cushman and his family were among them.

Beginning in 1617, Cushman spent much of his time in England in preparation for a voyage to America. Elder William Brewster was in hiding for publishing religious materials opposing King James I. The Pilgrims looked to Cushman and John Carver to pick up where Brewster had left off in negotiating with London investors to fund the crossing.

Robert Cushman

By June 1619, Cushman and Carver had secured a patent from the Virginia Company for a tract of land in northern Virginia and passage on the Mayflower. As purchasing agents for the Leyden congregation, the men began to secure food and supplies.

In Holland a smaller ship, the Speedwell, was hired, and it sailed for Southampton to join the Mayflower. On the way, it took on water. After failed attempts to repair the vessel, it was finally declared unseaworthy for the long, treacherous voyage.

After more than a month of delays, the Mayflower, overcrowded with one hundred two passengers plus crew, set sail on September 16, 1620.

Prior to sailing, Robert Cushman became seriously ill and was advised not to attempt the crossing. A year later, shortly after the first Thanksgiving, Cushman, his fourteen-year-old son Thomas, and thirty-three others arrived in Plymouth Colony aboard a smaller vessel, the *Fortune*.

With no ordained minister among the settlers, Cushman, a deacon, delivered the following message to the Plymouth Church on December 6, 1621. His message, titled *The Sin and Danger of Self-Love,* is the earliest documented sermon preached in America.

And you, my loving friends, the Adventurers to
this Plantation, as your care has been first to settle
religion here before either profit or popularity, so, I
pray you, go on to do it much more, and be careful
to send godly men...I rejoice...that you thus honor
God with your riches, and I trust you shall be
repaid again double and treble in this world, yea,
and the memory of this action shall never die.

• • •

Leaving Thomas in the care of Governor William Bradford, Cushman returned to London in February 1622. He carried a journal, Mourt's Relation, describing in detail that first
year — the landing, exploration, and eventual settling of Plymouth Colony. It also recorded relations with the surrounding
Indians and the first Thanksgiving.

This journal is considered the most important historical
document of its kind in early American history. Its publica-
tion and distribution also served as a resource in England for
encouraging future emigration to the new colony.

Robert Cushman was an agent for the Plymouth Colony
and their investors until he died of the plague in London in
the spring of 1625 at age forty-eight. He was buried in Kent.

Early in 1626, on his return from England, Myles Standish
brought "notice of the death of their ancient friend, Mr. Cushman, whom the Lord took away also this year."

Governor Bradford, upon receiving notice of Cushman's
death, stated that he "was as their right hand with their friends
(London investors), and for divers years had done and conducted all their business with them to their great advantage."

Around 1636, Robert's son Thomas Cushman married
Mary Allerton of Leyden, and eight children were born to
them. He was ruling elder of the Plymouth Church in 1649

85

and remained in that office forty-two years until his death in December 1691. Mary died in Plymouth in November 1699, the last survivor of the Mayflower passengers.

Robert Cushman Monument

In 1855, family members erected a twenty-five foot monument to Robert Cushman and his descendants on Burial Hill in Plymouth, Massachusetts. The remains of Robert's son, Thomas, his wife, and other family members were located and reinterred beneath the monument.

• • •

Gilbert Cushman, a sixth generation descendant of Robert Cushman, was born in 1784 in Kent, New York. He wed Nancy Russell in 1805, and they were blessed with eleven children. Their eldest son Ira, born in 1806, chose as his wife Belinda Adams, also from Kent.

Members of Gilbert's extended family became part of the great western migration. Leaving Kent, they settled in Lima, Washtenaw County, in southern Michigan.

In his late twenties, Ira Cushman decided to undertake the long journey to Lima and seek out a suitable location for a new beginning. He decided on a one-hundred-seventy-four-acre tract about forty miles northwest of Lima and applied for a federal grant on September 28, 1836. Ira traveled back to

Kent and began preparations for life in the Michigan wilderness.

• • •

As a part of the larger Northwest Territory, the Michigan Territory was formed in 1805, and in 1837, Michigan became the twenty-sixth state. Property rights were not clearly defined until Indian treaties signed between 1819 and 1821, cleared land titles. Land offices were opened, and the early pioneers flooded in from New York and Pennsylvania.

The Michigan Territory grew more quickly than any other part of the United States. In 1820, not counting Indians, Michigan had fewer than nine thousand people. By 1840, the new state's population had reached more than two hundred thousand. Settlers were pouring into Michigan, doubling the population by 1850 and again by 1860. Farming was the state's primary economic activity.

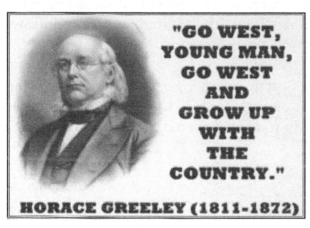

"GO WEST, YOUNG MAN, GO WEST AND GROW UP WITH THE COUNTRY."

HORACE GREELEY (1811-1872)

Horace Greely Quote Go West

Michigan also became more appealing when travel to the territory became less challenging. Originally, the only means of transportation was by horseback and wagon train. Steamships on Lake Erie and the Erie Canal greatly aided westward migration allowing faster, inexpensive travel by water.

The three-hundred-thirty-five-mile Erie Canal, opened in

1825, became the great highway from New England to the West. In the 1830s, signs on canal boats often read, "Flour, wool, and hides eastbound—farmers westbound."

The canal, stretching from Albany to Buffalo, was a small river with a depth and width of about four feet. Passengers traveled on flat-boats—large wooden boats with a cabin— pulled by teams of mules or horses walking along the edge of the canal. The flatboats traveled from two to four miles an hour depending on the pace of the team and congestion of canal traffic. The cost per passenger was about half a penny per mile.

During the day, passengers stayed on the boat's deck, and at night they slept in the cabin. The straw-padded bunks were often dirty and foul smelling. The cabin doors and windows were closed to keep out the mosquitoes—and the odor of the canal.

After reaching Buffalo, passengers boarded steamship lines for the three-day journey across Lake Erie to Detroit, the nearest big city. Early roads connected Detroit to the edge of the frontier.

• • •

In elementary music class, I enjoyed singing the Americana song, "Erie Canal," but I never could have imagined that the original settlers of our farm had traveled by this means.

I've got a mule, and her name is Sal, fifteen miles on the Erie Canal.
She's a good old worker and a good old pal, fifteen miles on the Erie Canal.
We've hauled some barges in our day, filled with lumber, coal and hay,
We know every inch of the way, from Albany to

Buffalo.
Low bridge, everybody down, low bridge, for we're
coming to a town.
And you'll always know your neighbor; you'll
always know your pal,
If you've ever navigated on the Erie Canal.

• • •

Ira's success in finding rich farmland and his enthusiasm about the opportunities in the Michigan Territory persuaded his parents and two of his brothers to join him. With the older children remaining in Kent, twenty-year-old Morris and four-teen-year-old George were eager to venture into the wilderness.

Ira, Belinda, and baby Mial, accompanied by his parents and brothers, arrived in Lima in February 1837. After purchasing a covered wagon, oxen, and a multitude of supplies, the family began the long journey to their new farm.

Getting there was a challenge. The roads were former Indian trails, full of rocks and holes, and often muddy. With no bridges, crossing even the smallest creek was a challenge. Losing the way, detouring around fallen trees and heavy underbrush, and eluding wild animals made for difficult travel.

Upon arrival, the men began felling trees to construct a sixteen by twenty-six foot log cabin and a shelter for

Bath sign on Clark Road near our house

89

the livestock. They planted corn, potatoes, and other garden crops that spring, and in the fall, seeded the land with winter wheat. They continued clearing land for additional crops.

Life on the frontier was very different from life in the city. The howling of wolves could be heard by night, and neighboring Indians might stop in by day.

• • •

That July, Ira's father Gilbert applied for a government patent for a parcel of land on Clark Road across Chandler. In the following years, Morris and George would purchase adjacent plats. Gilbert and his sons would thus own four farms in a row on the south side of Clark Road. Gilbert's property has remained in his family continually for more than one hundred seventy-five years.

Ira's patent was issued on September 28, 1837, for Section Nineteen in Bath Township. The purchase price was $1.25 per acre for a total of $218.35.

• • •

Soon after the Cushmans arrived, Nathaniel Newman settled with his family on the northeast corner of Clark and Chandler. His brother Joseph came soon after and began clearing land for a farm nearby. Joseph Newman died suddenly in 1838, the first death in Bath Township. Ira granted the family's request to bury their dead on his hill, directly across the road from the Newman's log cabin.

Ironically and tragically, Ira Cushman died the next June at the age of thirty-three. His young widow and her two small sons, Mial and Charles—the first white child born in Bath Township—stood with Ira's parents and brothers on that hill. The simple pine box was lowered into the grave, burying not only the remains of her husband, but also the dreams Belinda Cushman held for her future and the future of her sons.

The Cushman Cemetery would be a family burial ground for many years. Belinda remained a widow and raised her sons alone in a land inhabited almost entirely by Indians.

Chief Okemos

• • •

It has been stated by descendants of early pioneers that if it were not for the friendship of Indians, many settlers might not have survived the devastating hardships of frontier life. Their villages were located along the Looking Glass River, fewer than five miles north of the Cushman farms.

Chief Okemos was born in Shiawassee County around 1775. By the 1830s, he was recognized as a leader not only of the Saginaw Chippewa, but of many other Ojibwa bands who lived south of the Red Cedar River near present day East Lansing. The chief signed several treaties on behalf of his tribe.

From their camp on the Looking Glass, Okemos' braves traveled south to hunting grounds near present day Okemos, named for the chief. They were friendly and curious about these new settlers and were always welcome at the Cushman's door.

After Ira's death, Okemos' braves were especially kind to Belinda. Traveling back from a hunt, a few would stay behind and sleep on the cabin floor. Next morning they would chop firewood to last until the next trip through. They built a fence around the cabin to keep her children and livestock safe from wolves. These braves respected Belinda Cushman and repaid her friendship with needed help for the comfort and safety of her little family.

• • •

Belinda Cushman

During that period of history, wives and children were considered property of their husbands. Following Ira's death, Belinda made the fifteen-mile trip to St. Johns, the Clinton County seat of government. She filed papers legalizing her owner-ship of the farm and custody of her sons. In 1864, Belinda deeded the land to them, di-viding it equally into two eighty-seven-acre parcels. She lived with Charles and his family until her death at age eighty-five.

• • •

Today, an oral history of the Cushman family is only dim-ly remembered by their descendants. Growing up among the previous generation, I wish I had gathered and remembered more of their history. Thankfully, Harold Burnett's book, *The History of Bath Charter Township – 1826 to 1976* (now out of print) has provided much valuable information.

• • •

What was it like for Ira Cushman and his family to leave their home in Kent and travel to the Michigan wilderness? What hardships did they encounter along the way? Was life here better or worse than what they had expected?

Was the first log cabin constructed on the top of the hill where our farmhouse was built forty-two years later? Was the shelter for their livestock in the same place where our barn later stood?

Did they plant corn, potatoes and other garden crops that first spring in the same place we planted our garden?

What fears did Belinda Cushman experience when her husband died? How did he die? Could he have been saved in a more civilized setting? Did she consider going back to her home and family in Kent? How did she raise her sons alone in the wilderness? How much did she have to rely on Ira's family?

How? When? Where? Why? The questions go on.

In any case, for a brief time, Ira and Belinda Cushman lived and loved where my dad and mom lived and loved. Their sons Mial and Charles ran and played where Jack and I ran and played.

If only the land could tell their story — merely a hundred years before. Now that I'm more than three score and ten, a hundred years doesn't seem like a very long time.

• • •

Charles sold his farm to Joseph Drumheller in 1869. Joseph deeded it to his son Phillip in 1876, and he built our farmhouse three years later. The farm was sold again in 1925 to Carl Hollister, and we bought it from him in February 1940. Five years later we were able to buy the Armstrong farm, thus reuniting the two original halves after a period of sixty-six years.

• • •

Eventually, Dad converted the Armstrong farmhouse into two apartments, and Richard and my first home was in the upstairs. We later moved downstairs, and our first two sons were born there. We were away from Bath for six years due to my husband's work.

In 1961, Dad and Mom sold all of the land except the house, outbuildings, and some lots. They lived in the farmhouse for another twenty years.

When we returned to Bath, Dad and Mom gave us a lot around the corner from the farmhouse on Chandler Road. We built our house in 1966, and two more children were added to our family. We sold the house when we retired to Cedar Park, Texas, in May 2001. I had lived on the land as long as Belinda Cushman.

Dawn Voorheis Hawks

Chimney and ruins of the Kehoe farm

Chapter Seven-
ANDREW KEHOE

"Daddy, tell me again about that chimney."

"Dawn, that's all that's left of the Kehoe place."

"But why do they leave it like that? Why don't they tear it down? I don't like to look at it every time we go to Bath."

"Nobody'll clear it or work the land. They're afraid Kehoe planted more dynamite around the buildings and in the fields."

"Daddy, didn't something awful happen to Mrs. Kehoe?"

"Yes, he killed her before he burned the house and buildings."

"But Daddy, there's more, isn't there? The school—the children."

"Yes, Dawn, there's more. There's much more. . ."

• • •

May 18, 1927, started out as a perfect spring day. Twelve-year-old Iola Harte kissed her mother goodbye. "Don't worry if I don't come home at noon," she teased. "You know I have

97

to write tests today, and I might faint away!" Iola picked a bouquet of lilacs for her teacher as she hurried off.

Eight-year-old Arnie Bauerle didn't want to go to school that day. His parents and older sister and brother were going shoe shopping. Arnie had missed too many days of school with whooping cough, and he just couldn't miss another. There would be more shopping trips to Lansing.

Seven-year-old Ralph Cushman loved to play baseball. He was hitting a few balls when his mother called out that his sister Josephine was going to walk him to school. He protested, "But she doesn't have to take tests. Oh, all right, Mom. I'll be good."

• • •

Shortly before nine forty-five, east on Clark Road less than a mile from our farm, various incendiary devices planted in Andrew Kehoe's house and farm buildings began to explode. The homestead quickly erupted in roaring flames.

Almost simultaneously, a blast from carefully-placed explosives in the basement of the Bath Consolidated School devastated the north wing. The roof collapsed, killing thirty-eight children and two teachers. Iola, Arnie, and Ralph wouldn't return home that day.

About thirty minutes later, a Ford pickup loaded with dynamite and shrapnel exploded in front of the shattered school. The remains of Andrew Kehoe lay scattered among those of the innocents — the children of Bath — dead, dying, or wounded.

• • •

Andrew Kehoe was one of ten children born to Philip Kehoe. With his parents and six younger brothers, Philip came to this country about 1840 as part of the large Irish influx. The family settled in Maryland, and with new land opening up in the Michigan Territory, Philip headed west. He decided on Tecumseh, an area being populated by many other Irish immigrants.

With the security and promise of new land, Philip was ready to marry. He chose Mary Malone, who had been reared by an Irish Catholic priest. From the very beginning, the church was to be central to their home.

Tragedy soon struck when Mary died a week after giving birth to their second daughter. Philip remarried within a year, taking a second Mary for his wife. Four girls were born to this union and with the birth of each, Philip's disappointment grew. Finally, a son whom he named Andrew Philip was born on February 1, 1872. By the time Andrew reached his fifth birthday, his mother had borne three more children.

Shortly before or soon after the last child's birth, Mary Kehoe became seriously ill. As paralysis slowly devastated her body, she could no longer care for her family. She died when Andrew was eighteen.

Andrew chose to remain with his father, staking his future with the farm. But then, the unthinkable happened. Philip Kehoe, past sixty, took on a third wife—a comparably young widow with grown children. To add insult to injury, Philip presented Frances with a brand new brick house built directly across the road from the farmhouse.

• • •

Andrew's whereabouts for the next eight years are uncertain. Most likely, he followed up on his inventive and mechanical inclinations. Electricity was a natural for him. It was useful and powerful, and it could be destructive. He enrolled in an electrical school in St. Louis, Missouri, worked there as an electrician, and later became a lineman in Iowa.

Sometime around 1905, Philip could no longer work the farm due to progressive arthritis. Andrew returned home, lived in the old farmhouse, and took over for his father. In the next few years, he enrolled in some agricultural short courses at Michigan State College.

Andrew managed the farm well, adjusting his methods to the times and continuing its prosperity. He introduced the use of explosives for clearing the land. It was an experience in destruction — harmless destruction — but it was like a new toy.

Philip Kehoe was approaching seventy and in failing health. Andrew worked from dawn to dusk with the knowledge that the family farm would not pass to him.

• • •

On September 17, 1911, Frances Kehoe returned to her kitchen to prepare lunch after picking up hickory nuts in the nearby woods. Using a match, she attempted to light the burner on the gasoline stove. Suddenly, there was a flash explosion followed by agonizing screams. Although Frances was standing on a rug, there was no attempt to put it around her. Instead, Andrew doused her with water — only spreading the flames. The fire was subdued, and Frances, in agony, was carried to her bed.

Andrew went down the road to the Murphy farm. "Hettie, would you call Dr. Tuttle?" Although Andrew didn't give the least appearance of alarm, Hettie was concerned. "Is someone sick?"

"No, Fannie got burned. Would you come and help?" Almost as an afterthought, he added, "Would you call the priest, too?"

Hettie was stunned when she saw her friend. Frances' skin was completely blackened, and all she could manage to say was, "Hettie, Hettie!"

100

The doctor and priest arrived about the same time, as fast as horse and buggy could carry them. They quickly determined that this was more a case for the priest than the doctor. The family collie kept a moaning vigil outside the bedroom window, and a few hours later, Frances Kehoe died.

There had been talk about problems lighting the stove, and it was determined that this was merely a tragic accident. Only years later, after the horrific events of May 18, did speculation turn to Andrew's fascination with destruction—of anything and anyone he deemed standing in his way.

• • •

Now in his early forties, Andrew resumed an old courtship with Ellen Price whom he'd reportedly met at Michigan State years before. The two had briefly dated before Andrew left for St. Louis.

Nellie's background was similar to Andrew's. Born in 1875, she was the daughter of Irish Catholic immigrants, Patrick and Mary Ann Price. Patrick moved his family from Lansing to the farm near Bath owned by his brother, Lawrence.

Her mother died when Nellie was just eighteen, and since her father didn't remarry, she assumed the burden of mothering the younger children. In 1908, Patrick moved back to Lansing where his children could be closer to his family. Nellie was thirty-one when the last child reached sixteen.

Six years later, Nellie Price wed Andrew Kehoe on May 14, 1912. Philip Kehoe gave his son and his bride use of the old homestead. The warm and attractive Nellie was an immediate hit, not only with the family, but with the neighbors as well.

Rather abruptly, however, something of a withdrawal took place, and it may have been related to Andrew's break with the church. When the original parish church was torn down, the Kehoe's assessment for the new sanctuary was four hundred dollars. One of the parish priests called at their home to collect, and he was ordered off the property. Andrew never returned to church, and it was said that he wouldn't allow his wife to attend.

• • •

Less than a year after his wife's death and three months after Andrew's marriage, Philip Kehoe wrote his will. Upon his death the farm was to be sold and the proceeds divided among his ten children and two grandchildren. Andrew's aspirations for remaining on the family farm were shattered. Philip died in 1915, and Andrew proceeded to follow his father's request. The family farm was put up for sale.

• • •

In 1917, Nellie's Uncle Lawrence died, leaving a considerable estate with money going to a variety of relatives and charities.

Andrew and Nellie Kehoe

The eighty-acre Price farm in Bath, Nellie's childhood home, was still in the family. The farm was a showcase for the region. The three-story house was finished in oak throughout and equipped with a furnace, lighting plant, and pressure tanks that provided water on all three floors. The land was rich, and a lush woodlot lay to the east. Andrew put six thousand dollars down and carried a six-thousand-dollar mortgage.

The Kehoes were active in social events and became members of the Friday Afternoon Club. Some people remembered Nellie from her youth, growing up on the Price farm. Andrew became respected in the community for his growing interest in local affairs and willingness to volunteer his time. Yet some people seemed to see a darker side to his nature.

A typical one-room school

Chapter Eight-
MAYDAY

"It seemed as though the floor went up several feet. After the first shock, I thought for a moment I was blind. The air seemed to be full of children and flying desks and books. Children were tossed high in the air; some were catapulted out of the building." First grade teacher Bernice Sterling recounted the explosion as being like a terrible earthquake.

"I don't remember hearing any noise, but I remember flying in the air and seeing things fly between me and the sun," recalled Ada Belle Dolton McGonigal, a fifth-grader at the time. "But I don't ever remember falling."

• • •

In 1840, Peter Finch built a log structure in the southeast section of the township for his wife, a school teacher who saw a need to educate the local children. No more than ten generally attended — mostly girls — as the pioneers believed their boys could get all the education they needed on the family farm. Between 1845 and 1887, nine more schools were built.

In spite of the advantages of a neighborhood school, the one-room school had some glaring inadequacies. Teachers received minimal salaries and were required to perform additional duties besides teaching eight different grades. They kept the school house clean, carried water from the school pump or neighboring well, and in cold weather, arrived early to build the fire. Most boarded with students' families or other locals.

With a severe shortage of qualified teachers in the state, those willing to endure the hardships of a one-room school considerably narrowed the pool.

• • •

The Bath Village School was built in 1858 as a log structure and was replaced by a two-story brick building in 1873. Offering ten grades, the attendance rose to one hundred twenty-five by 1879. This school met the needs of village children and those living close by, but most were on farms scattered throughout the township.

The people of Bath wanted something more for their children, and the answer was consolidation. It would provide better facilities with competent teachers and the opportunity to attend high school. Children would be safely bused from the moment they left home until they returned.

In spite of sharp dissention in the township, the 1921 vote for consolidation passed. The Village School building would become part of the new structure.

The Bath Consolidated School opened in 1922 with twelve grades. There were six motor-driven buses and one with a pot-bellied stove drawn by a team of horses. Emory E. Huyck was hired as the first superintendent, and the student population that year was two hundred thirty-six.

Consolidation brought a whole new way of life. The sight of the green buses became expected and anticipated, either on the back country roads or on the unpaved main roads.

Life in the village had changed as well. Aside from the superintendent, principal, and shop teacher, the entire faculty was ladies. For the most part, they were young and fresh out of teacher-training schools. They lived in a boarding house on Main Street and enjoyed walking in the village or out into the surrounding countryside.

• • •

From the very beginning, Andrew Kehoe voiced his opposition to consolidation. In 1923, the school board bought five acres of land for an athletic field and installed a new lighting plant. Kehoe's rage intensified as his taxes increased.

During the next two years, Kehoe insinuated to some of his neighbors that if he were on the school board, he would cut expenses. At an annual board meeting in 1924, he was chosen to fill an unexpired three-year term and was appointed treasurer. His books were always satisfactory, but he had signifi-

The Bath Consolidated School

cant difficulties getting along with the other board members. At meetings, he seemed unwilling to compromise, and if he did not get his way, he moved to adjourn.

Kehoe's dislike of Superintendent Huyck was evident from the beginning. He invariably voted against any of Huyck's pay raises. On one occasion, the superintendent requested a summer vacation, and Kehoe argued against it. When he saw that the other board members were in favor, he moved to give him one week.

In the spring of 1926, Kehoe was defeated in his bid for township clerk. Since he was so antagonistic on the school board, people were wary of giving him a seat on the township board. His resentment toward the people of Bath was mounting.

• • •

Because of his large, modern house with substantial barns, outbuildings, and farm implements, Kehoe's taxes were among the highest in the school district. He blamed failed attempts to get the valuation lowered and complained that he had paid too much for the farm in the first place. Kehoe stopped making mortgage payments to the Price Estate and let his fire insurance lapse.

As an heir of her uncle, Nellie received legacy payments. After a while, the executors began applying these funds to the mortgage payments. Kehoe took the matter to court, and Nellie continued to receive the checks.

The beneficiaries of the Price estate included hospitals, Catholic and industrial schools, and various other charities. After failing to negotiate a payment plan, the executors' only recourse was to begin foreclosure proceedings.

Nellie's hopes of maintaining family ties and remaining on her childhood homestead came to a crashing halt when

Kehoe's plan of playing on the sympathies of her relatives failed.

• • •

Kehoe was a very competent electrician. During the summer of 1926, he was asked to do repairs and rewiring of the school. He was given a key and had free access to the building.

• • •

Kehoe's neighbors called him the "dynamite farmer." Using explosives to blow up stumps and rocks in his fields, Kehoe began buying up huge stockpiles.

On New Year's Eve, 1927, massive explosions rocked the area, and bright flashes lit up the Kehoe farm. When asked about it later, Kehoe said that he had wired a timing device to dynamite and set it to go off at midnight.

• • •

Nellie had been in poor health for some time, and her condition continued to decline. Plagued with nagging headaches and severe coughing, she was in and out of St. Lawrence Hospital—named after her Uncle Lawrence Price—throughout the winter of 1927.

Andrew Kehoe's life seemed to be falling apart: impending foreclosure, Nellie's health, dashed political ambition, and constant opposition with the school board and the superintendent. He seemed to quit farming, and his neighbors wondered as his crops rotted in the fields. But Kehoe was not idle. He began executing his horrendous plans of revenge.

• • •

On May 1, Ida Hall moved into a house on Main Street

next to the school. She frequently heard the sound of a vehicle driving to and from the school late at night. On one occasion, she saw a Ford pickup parked close by the front steps, and twice the driver carried objects inside. During this same time, Kehoe's neighbors noticed the almost nightly trips toward Bath.

On Monday night, May 16, Kehoe completed setting the explosives in the basement of the school. His timing devices were manual alarm clocks rigged to complete the deadly circuit at the selected time — soon after school began. Nothing short of a miracle could now save the school. Kehoe had chosen a fate worse than death itself for his fancied enemies — the destruction of their children.

• • •

Kehoe had also formulated plans for his revenge on the Price family. During Nellie's lengthy hospital stay, he planted dynamite attached to electrical wires throughout the house. The neighbors noticed him stringing lines to his outbuildings. He carried straw into his tool shed and put a timing device in the chicken coop. What the dynamite did not destroy, the subsequent fire would.

Kehoe needed more time. He was relieved when Nellie's sisters asked if she could recuperate a few more days with them. On Tuesday evening, May 17, Kehoe brought her home.

The decision that his wife must die that night had been planned well in advance. The method was simple — a sharp blow to the head. Kehoe laid her body on a hog cart, covered it with old carpeting, and hid it behind the chicken coop.

All of Kehoe's horrific plans were now in place — even his suicide, accomplished with a rifle shot to ignite the dynamite in his pickup. Perhaps he even thought he could take out some of his enemies with him. His timing was carefully calculated — Wednesday, May 18 — two days before the end of the school year.

• • •

As his house and buildings exploded, engulfing the farmstead in roaring flames, Kehoe got into his pickup and drove toward Bath.

Shortly thereafter, at nine forty-five, the blast in the basement of the north wing rocked the entire building, blowing away the main entrance and the stairway. Buckled floors and blown out walls sent the roof crashing down on the remains of the first floor classrooms, burying third- through sixth-grade children and their teachers.

The sound of the explosion was heard for miles, and townspeople and parents rushed to the scene. Grief-stricken, they tore at the wreckage in search of their boys and girls, many of whom could not hear the sound of frantic voices calling their names.

The north wing of the school

Several people recognized Kehoe as he slowly passed the school. What had gone wrong? Only the north wing was down. All of those explosives should have brought down the entire building and buried all two hundred students.

Kehoe drove to the end of Main

111

Street, turned west on Sleight Road and continued down Chandler and Clark Roads, passing his blazing farmstead. He pulled up in front of the school and surveyed the bystanders. There might be a chance to annihilate his adversary.

Superintendent Huyck was just returning from the telephone office after requesting emergency medical and rescue aid. Kehoe called him over to his pickup and detonated the dynamite. Two other bystanders were also killed — along with an eight-year-old boy who had wandered out of the wreckage. Several others were severely injured by flying shrapnel.

A temporary morgue, sectioned off on the school lawn, continued to grow. Grief-stricken parents peered under bloody sheets praying they would not find the child they were seeking.

• • •

Mrs. Eugene Hart sat on the grass with a little dead girl on each side. She was holding an injured boy who would soon die. Vivian and Percy were in third grade, and Iola was in sixth grade. Seventeen-year-old Perry, gravely injured in the truck blast, would spend many months in the hospital.

Octa Harte slowly walked up to a nearby group of people. With downcast eyes, he uttered, "I've lost my boy." He paused and went on. "But Eugene Hart has lost three of his youngsters, and another badly hurt. It must be hard on Gene." This devastated father hesitated to regain control. "Galen was a mighty fine boy if I do say so myself. I'm certainly going to miss him. I just wanted to tell someone." Galen Harte, age twelve, was added to the list of dead.

• • •

Hundreds of people worked in the wreckage all day. Besides townspeople and parents, many outsiders, firefighters and police officers from Lansing, rushed to the scene.

Upon arrival, Michigan State Police halted rescue work until examination of the south wing basement was completed. More than five hundred pounds of explosive materials along with an alarm clock were removed. Investigators speculated that the initial explosion may have caused a short circuit, failing to set off the other round of bombs.

Dr. Crum and his wife — a nurse — set up their pharmacy on Main Street as a triage center. More doctors and nurses, as well as the American Red Cross, began arriving from Lansing and surrounding areas. The most severely injured were sent by ambulance to hospitals in Lansing, and private automobiles transported the lesser injured and parents.

As soon as the coroner arrived, the dead were removed to the town hall. Later in the day, ambulances transported their remains to area undertakers as designated by the parents.

• • •

Thirty-eight elementary students, two teachers, the superintendent, and two townspeople were among the dead. More than fifty were injured, many seriously.

The incalculable trauma to surviving children, families, and rescuers would linger for decades — and for some, a lifetime.

The Bath School Disaster stood as the deadliest mass murder in our country's history for sixty-eight years. That death toll was exceeded when one hundred sixty-eight were killed in the Oklahoma City Federal Building bombing in 1995. At that time, journalists arrived in Bath to interview survivors, and the nation was reminded of the tragedy.

Andrew Kehoe had completed his vengeance and attained infamy. Newspapers across the country once again characterized him as maniac, madman, and fiend.

Memorial Plaque

Chapter Nine- CARLTON HOLLISTER

"Hello. Oh, Helen, how are you?"

"Hi, Dawn, we're fine. I just had to call and tell you what happened last weekend when Bob and I were visiting my sister up north. After church we got to talking with another couple, the Hollisters. Mr. Hollister said he grew up on a farm near Bath, and I told him our daughter-in-law's mother did, too. Can you believe it's the same farm?"

"That's amazing, Helen. Yes, we bought the farm from the Hollisters in 1940."

"And Dawn, that's not all. Mr. Hollister was in the Bath School disaster. After all these years, he's decided to write down his recollections. He's going to send me a copy, and I'll pass it on to you."

• • •

Carlton Hollister's account from his personal experiences, dated May 18, 1997, on the seventieth anniversary of the disaster:

> On that eventful morning of May 18, 1927, we, the students in the fifth grade of the Bath Consolidated School, assembled in our regular classroom on the ground floor in the northwest corner of the building.
>
> During the year, our homeroom teacher Mrs. Blanche Harte had been instructing the sixth grade class in one particular subject. This was examination time, and arrangements had been made for us to exchange rooms with the sixth graders so they could write their exam in our room. As we fifth graders marched up the stairs in single file, we met our friends coming down. What no one ever suspected was that this would be, for many, the last time on earth we would ever meet.
>
> As we entered the classroom, I selected a seat near the center and settled down beside Lloyd, one of my classmates. Miss Eva Gubbins, the sixth grade teacher, walked down the aisle with a hand full of papers and sat down to read and grade them just behind my friend in the next row. Being curious as to whose seat I was sitting in, I pulled a book from the desk and found that it belonged to Galen Harte. He was a year older than I, a good friend, and we were in the same Sunday school class at church.
>
> Some seconds later, we came crashing down on those sixth graders, and Galen died, perhaps in the very place where I would normally have been sitting.
>
> When the blast occurred, I do not remember hearing any noise or feeling any shock, but mercifully, I lost

consciousness. I gradually woke up some time later on the porch of the telephone office downtown, a block and a half away from the school. The telephone switchboard was one front room in a private dwelling.

The telephone wires from the surrounding area led into the control station where a real live operator would connect your phone line manually with whatever local or long distance line you might request.

As I gradually regained consciousness, I could hear Lenora Babcock, the seventeen-year-old switchboard operator repeat her frantic message out over the telephone system. "The school has been blown up! We need help. People are dead and injured. Many are trapped in the wreckage."

From what she was telling them, I gradually began to understand some of what had happened. Because my mind was dull, my head hurting, my body bruised and weary, I had no real sense of time.

It was some time later that I recognized my mother by my side. She lived twenty years after that day, and I never asked, nor did she ever tell how she found me. She did ask if I felt able to walk a little.

Someone had suggested that I be moved a half block or so down the street to the teachers' rooming house. They had a couch on the front porch on which I could lay and where there was less traffic. We made it to the new location and rested there for a short time.

Mother than asked if I could try to move again, perhaps to the family car parked on the south part of town. I said "yes," but I didn't want to go by the school. There was no other way to reach the car my father had driven to town with my mother and oldest brother. She told me we would be on the lower side of the street, and she would protect me from the terrible view.

117

We hadn't walked very far beyond the school when a kind stranger asked if he could give us a ride in his car to where we wanted to go. Mother accepted the offer so she could leave our car for my father to have when he would be free to come home after helping with the rescue work. The man said he was a salesman going by and wanted to be of help to someone. This was only one of many ways people came together to help meet the needs of Bath folks in whatever way they could that day and in the days that followed.

So at home, Mother gently washed away the blood and plaster dust from my head, cleaned me up, and thanked God for bringing our family through this tragic day.

My younger brother Robert, a second grader, was in the south end of the building and able to escape with his teacher and classmates through a hole in the wall.

I stayed in bed for several days and read in the newspaper about what had happened. I pondered over the list of children and adults who were injured and of those who died and wondered why our family had been spared from death or serious injury.

For some reason we didn't talk about the experience from then on. It was seldom mentioned in our family or among the survivors or in the community in the years that followed.

I always wondered how I was removed from the building and why and by whom I was carried to the telephone office. About five years ago, I expressed my question to my oldest brother Kenneth for the first time. He said he knew. Mr. Huyck, the school superintendent, carried me there when he went down to the telephone office to send out calls for help. Others have said that I was the first live but injured body removed from the wreckage. Mr. Huyck died a few minutes later when Kehoe blew up his car.

Three days after that fateful Wednesday, I was up and around. It was Sunday, May 22, and on that day, according to some police estimates, perhaps as many as one hundred thousand automobiles filled with curious and sympathetic spectators passed through the village of Bath.

The Hollister farmstead is on Clark Road about a mile west of the Kehoe farm and two miles west of Bath village and school. The state police had designated Clark Road as the principal highway for one-way traffic into the area. From early morning until late afternoon, the cars came bumper to bumper, stop and go, in a solid line often five miles long.

Sometime later, Mrs. Harte, Galen's mother, came to my parents with a proposal. They had a Shetland pony for their boy. He dearly loved the animal, and they were together as often as they were able. Now, Galen was dead, and his younger brother was a bit too young for the horse. The presence of the pony was a daily reminder of their loss, and it seemed that healing might be easier if it would be out of sight for a while.

Would I like to take the pony and his equipment for the summer? Needless to say, I felt honored by their offer, but at the same time humbled. I was reminded daily that by sitting in Galen's seat at school, I had been spared from death or serious injury. Now I was to be privileged to sit in his saddle and enjoy the blessing he had left behind. The horse and I spent many precious hours together that summer.

When school started in the fall, Mother wanted me to go and live with her sister in Flint. I tried it for a week but was too lonesome for home to manage.

The sixth grade met on the second floor of the Community Hall on Main Street that year. Some of the classmates were still under treatment for injuries, and many were missing. But those of us who remained and were able proceeded to learn as we were taught.

We were able to move back into the rebuilt school with its new gymnasium in the fall of 1928. Our class of thirteen, with several new members, graduated in the spring of 1934.

• • •

We moved to the Hollister farm thirteen years after the school disaster. Carlton's house became my house. If only the walls could tell his story: pain and healing, guilt and grief, strength and courage, and praise and thanksgiving.

Dawn Voorheis Hawks

First and Second Grade Classrooms

Chapter Ten-
ANN WHITNEY

"Dawn, how nice of you to call. Thank you for sending the birthday card. It took us a while to figure out how to work it. I didn't know they made singing cards."

"Well, Ann, since you can't read anymore, I thought it would be fun for you to hear 'Happy Birthday.' Turning ninety is a big deal. Did you have a party?"

"Yes, John came, and we had pizza and cake."

"That's really nice. John is such a good nephew. Ann, I've decided to write my memories of growing up in Bath. Over the years you've mentioned a time or two about being in the school disaster and your husband Orb using his ladder to get children out. But I've never heard your story. Would you tell me?"

"Lots of people have asked me over the years, and I wouldn't talk to them. But, Dawn, we've been neighbors and friends for a long time. Yes, I'll tell you my story."

• • •

The following is Ann's account of the events:

Both the kindergarteners and we first graders were in the same class, and Miss Sterling was our teacher. The school year was almost over, and we didn't have to take tests like when we were older. Our workbooks were mostly done so our teacher had planned some of our favorite things to do. We really loved hearing stories.

We had gone through our opening activities. Miss Sterling told us the name of the story she was going to read, and we hurried to get around her desk.

She had just started to read when all of a sudden there was this whoosh! The blast in the basement made the floor come up, and everything in the room was flying around — desks, chairs, books — and us children. Chunks of the ceiling were falling down. We couldn't hardly see for all the plaster dust. We were screaming and crying and trying to get up.

Then Miss Sterling could hear the principal Mr. Huggett calling out. The janitors, one-armed Lyn Harrington and Frank Smith, were with him. Mr. Huggett said to come out, walk down the hall, and go out the back door. "Get away from the school."

Miss Sterling sounded very stern. She told us to stop crying and be quiet.

"Children, come here, come right now. Hold somebody's hand. Walk — don't run. Follow me and stay close."

Mary Jean Dryer took my hand. She kept saying, "Annie, don't leave me."

I told her I wouldn't. "Hurry, Mary Jean. We got to follow Miss Sterling."

We did what Mr. Huggett said. We all got out, and we followed Miss Sterling away from the school. We were so scared, and we huddled around her. She tried her best to comfort us and told us to check and see if we were hurt. I looked down, and there was blood on my hand. Then I looked all over to see where I was bleeding, but I couldn't find any place.

Mary Jean gasped, "Annie, my hand!" For the first time I looked at her. Her head was cut, and blood was running down the side of her face and getting on her arm and hand. We dabbed at it with a hanky.

The second grade classroom was right next to the part where the upper classrooms came down. Miss Gutekunst had her children in the back of the room, reading them a story. Part of the brick wall fell onto the front part of the room. If they'd been sitting at their desks, half of them would have been buried. Mr. Huggett had to break a hole through the wall to get the children into our room. He took Miss Gutekunst and her students over to where we were. Then he went round to the front of the school.

Mary Jean's big sister Arlene was in the south wing. As soon as she could get out, she came running. She picked up Mary Jean, hugged her tight, both of them crying and headed for home.

The mothers who lived in town came first, running and looking so scared. They knew what part of the school their child was in. When the children saw their mothers or fathers, they ran to each other. There was such crying and hugging as they hurried away.

It took a while for the parents who lived out in the country to come. But one by one our class and the second graders got less and less.

And then I was the only one. Miss Sterling took me around to the front of the school. A lady was standing there looking like she didn't know how to help. When she saw Miss Sterling all covered with plaster dust and about to fall over, she told her to get away and find some place to rest. She said she'd try to find someone who knew me and could take me home.

Now I could see how really terrible it was. People were clawing at the wreckage under the roof—arms and legs and heads sticking out all covered with dust and blood.

Some children were walking around not knowing what to do or where to go. Parents were running around calling out names and asking if anyone had seen their boy or girl. Hurt children were scattered on the grass with parents and others tending to them the best they could. Off to one side, dead children were being laid out in a row—covered with sheets so only their feet stuck out. There was a lot of screaming and crying over there.

The upper grades were in the south wing. Those on the first floor were climbing out through the broken windows, but those on the second floor were trapped. People were yelling at them not to jump, but some did. They brought as many ladders as they could find.

My future husband Orb was painting at Joe Perrone's house. He ran over and used his ladder to get students and teachers down, and then he worked in the wreckage.

The lady was so nice. She took my hand and asked me why my parents weren't there to get me. I told her my ma died when I was two and my pa was at home and that we lived out in the country. She asked me my name, and I told her Annie Cipo.

She said, "We got to get you away from here. Come with me, Annie. Let's see if somebody knows you."

I told her I didn't want to look at those children. "Oh, that boy's leg's bleeding something awful!"

"They're trying to help him, Annie. Put your face against my skirt and don't look." We started walking around again with her calling out, "Does anyone know this child?"

Some folks looked up, but they just shook their head. After a while the lady said "Annie, we got to try something different. We'll walk around, and you tell me if you see anybody you know." We had to go past hurt children, but we stayed away from where they were covered with sheets.

After a few more minutes, I saw Eddie Drumheller. We walked toward him, and he said "Oh, Annie, I'm so glad to see you. You all right? There's blood on your arm."

"That's from Mary Jean Dryer. Her head was bleeding, and I guess it got on me."

The lady seemed relieved. "Mr. Drumheller, you're the first person who knows this child. Would you see to it that she gets home?"

"Well, I'll be glad to ma'am, if I can get somebody to take me home. See my car over there next to Kehoe's truck? That's all that's left of it."

I sat in the back seat feeling so alone. Mr. Drumheller and his neighbor were talking about Mr. Kehoe killing all those children.

I kept thinking they were going to forget me. We got almost down to Drumheller Road, and Mr. Drumheller said, "Oh, I almost forgot. We've got to take Annie home. We can drop her off at Stoll Road."

After my sisters grew up and moved away, it was just Pa and me living in our log cabin. Pa was from the old country, and we kind of kept to ourselves. Pa didn't know nothing about Kehoe's trouble with his taxes and the school board and nothing else that went on in town.

We usually kept four or five cows, and the Wilson Dairy truck picked up milk at all the farms every day. For a couple of years, the winters had been really bad, and the truck could only get down Clark Road. With him living on Clark, Kehoe said Pa could drop off milk at his place. We used our horse and sleigh and went down Drumheller to pick up milk cans from a couple of other farmers. The Kehoes were so nice. Mrs. Kehoe even came out on the porch and talked to me.

When they dropped me off at my corner, I ran home as fast as I could. Pa was working out in the barn. "Annie, why're you running like that? Stop crying! Tell me what happened."

Eddie Drumheller's car

"Oh, Pa, it was so terrible. There was this bang! The school shook something awful. The ceiling was falling down. We followed Miss Sterling out. There was screaming and crying. Oh, Pa, so many children. They put the dead ones on the grass with sheets over them."

"Annie, Annie, slow down! Come here, child. Now tell me what happened."

"The roof came down, Pa. Mr. Drumheller said Mr. Kehoe blew up the school."

"Blew up the school! Oh, Annie, that can't be right. He wouldn't do that. Somethin' else musta' happened. Or somebody else musta' done it. Not Mr. Kehoe. Mr. Kehoe's a nice man."

Girl with a cat

Chapter Eleven-
AFTERMATH

"Shirley, I interviewed Ann Whitney about the school disaster for my memoirs. She talked about her friend Mary Jean Dryer. When we were growing up, your grandparents lived in that big brick house on Clark Road just west of Main Street. If I remember right, their name was Dryer. Could Mary Jean be any relation to you?"

"Why, yes, Dawn. Mary Jean was my mother's little sister. The high school students were on the second floor of the south wing, and Mama wasn't hurt. As soon as she could get out, she found Mary Jean in back of the school with her class and took her home.

"Daddy was also in the school, but he wasn't hurt either. He was worried about Mama and kept asking people if they had seen Arlene. He was very relieved when someone told him that she and Mary Jean were all right, and that they had walked home.

"Daddy worked in that awful rubble all day. He was president and valedictorian of the class of 1927. He had his speech all written. But you know they didn't get to graduate. Daddy never talked about that terrible day."

• • •

Shirley Robson Hanna is my dearest friend, our kinship beginning in kindergarten and continuing through the years. Until my polio scare, I had planned on attending nursing school with her at St. Lawrence Hospital. Even though we spent so much time together, it was only after Ann Whitney mentioned Mary Jean Dryer that I questioned Shirley about the disaster.

"Daddy didn't talk about it." That was pretty much the way it was with the people of Bath. Immeasurable, unspeakable wounds were best left covered and never exposed to the light of day.

Parents didn't talk about it, and the next generation knew little — unless there were recurring visits to small graves. Except for the little girl with the kitten, the entire event might have been lost to us.

I began kindergarten at James Couzens Agricultural School in 1942. One of the first things that fascinated me was the life-size statue in the hall facing the main entrance. We were told that the girl was a memorial to all the children who died in the Bath School Disaster. She appears to be light-hearted, a tribute to the little lives that should have remained free of care.

We were much older when we finally understood. The statue wasn't made from melted-down pennies contributed by Michigan school children. Rather, the pennies funded the crafting of the sculpture by University of Michigan professor, Carlton W. Angel.

• • •

It has been stated that if you didn't have a loved one killed or injured in the disaster, your neighbor did. The more I learned about this tragedy just thirteen years before we

132

moved to Bath, the closer I felt to those who lived through that horrendous time.

• • •

Carlton Hollister's farm became my farm. He helped his father in the barn where I helped my dad. He stabled Galen Harte's pony where I stabled Prince, and we rode down the same lane to the back woodlot.

Galen's mother, Mrs. Shirley Harte, was one of my Sunday school teachers at the Bath Methodist Church. Another teacher, Aletha Fredrick Stanlake, was a third grader when the disaster occurred. Her class sustained the highest death toll—ten of sixteen. One of three injured, Mrs. Stanlake crawled through a hole to escape the wreckage. Her father, Frankie Fredrick, was one of our favorite school bus drivers.

As a teenager I sang in the Methodist Church choir with Sim Ewing. We entered the sanctuary each Sunday morning wearing long robes and singing "Holy, Holy, Holy." My kindergarten teacher, Viva Cushman, led the way to the choir loft, and Mr. Ewing always came last. He was Bath Township Supervisor for nearly twenty years and owner of Ewing's Grocery. At the sound of the blast, Mr. Ewing ran from his store and was one of the first to arrive on the scene. His son Earl was one of twelve killed in the sixth grade class of twenty-eight. Another son Don, a senior, was unhurt.

Mr. Ewing worked with the Red Cross raising funds for hospital and funeral expenses. After turning over ownership of the grocery to his son, he became an insurance agent. He wrote the policy on my husband Richard's first car, a 1934 Chevy.

Besides buying our groceries and renting frozen food locker space at Ewing's, we often went to the R & R Hardware named for Rounds and Reasoner. At the time of the disaster,

Jack Rounds was in the fifth grade and fell from the second floor with Carlton Hollister. Lee Reasoner, one of the eleven injured sixth graders, was on the first floor. Both boys were pulled from the rubble with cuts and fractures.

Abbot and Ave Sweet Nelson owned Nelson's General Store. Mrs. Nelson was buried in the rubble with Lillian Reed Wildt, another sixth grader. The girls could hear rescuers working above them and began screaming. The digging continued until they were brought out.

Ava's younger brother Dean, also in the sixth grade, appeared lifeless and was lying among the dead when someone noticed signs of life. After enduring a long hospital stay, Dean's parents were told to keep him in bed and not expect him to live very long.

One morning Dean looked out the window and saw his father plowing with their team of horses. He quickly got dressed, went out to the field, and began picking up rocks. When his dad turned around and started back in his direction, he looked up and shouted, "Son, what are you doing out here?"

Dean shouted back, "Dad, if I'm going to die, I'm going to die doing what I want to do. And what I want to do is what I'm supposed to do. And that's follow you and pick up the rocks."

Dean Sweet continued to be a prominent citizen of the Bath community until his death at age ninety-two.

• • •

My mother was a member of the Sunbeam Rebekah Lodge. These ladies were her closest friends, but the ones who bore horrific memories never spoke of them.

Virgaline Zeeb was among the neighbors who rushed to Kehoe's flaming farm. Some furniture had already been carried out when a cache of dynamite was sighted in the living room. Orders were given to clear out, and the sounds of the exploding school sent them all rushing to Bath.

Adabelle Dolton McGonigal, a sixth grade student, worked at the Bath post office for many years. She was nearly blown out of the building, and amazingly only suffered cuts and bruises. Her son Johnnie and I were classmates from kindergarten through high school.

Mable Hunter was one of my mother's dearest friends. She sang at fifth-grade teacher Blanche Harte's funeral held in the Harte home. After teaching in rural schools, Blanche Beuhler had married Roscoe Harte, a local farmer, and moved to Bath. She was greatly loved by her students and admired for her conscientious work in school, church, and community activities.

• • •

We neighbored with LaVere and Florence Harte who lived across the road from the Kehoe's. Dad had learned to cut hair as a boy and cut his brother and father's hair. Every few weeks, Mr. Harte would come over. He appreciated the free haircut, and both men enjoyed the conversation.

In addition to losing their sister-in-law Blanche, the Harte's fourth-grade son Robert was among the dead. Rev. Scott McDonald, pastor of the Bath Methodist Church, conducted Robert's service on Saturday afternoon. The morning before, the McDonalds had buried their eldest daughter Thelma, a third grader.

Dad and George Hall liked to talk farming, and I would sometimes go with Dad to their place. We never knew that the Halls had lost their two older children, Willa Marie, in the fifth grade, and George, Jr., in the third grade.

• • •

Besides Johnnie McGonigal, another classmate was Betty Vail Stull. At the beginning of each school year, some of the teachers seated us in alphabetical order until they memorized our names. It was always "Betty Vail, Dawn Voorheis." Betty's mother, Josephine Cushman Vail, had walked her little brother Ralph, a third grader, to school that morning. Ralph's body was one of the last to be found in the wreckage.

Walter Kyes and I went through school together. He and Richard were football and basketball teammates, and he was best man at our wedding in 1956. His mother, Alice Webster Kyes, class of 1927, was my winter 4-H leader, and Walt's grandfather, Melvin Kyes, was Kehoe's chief antagonist on the school board.

• • •

My parents Arthur and Lillian Voorheis, and Richard's parents Harold and Mary Rose Crouse are buried in Pleasant Hill Cemetery. Although victims were laid to rest in several other cemeteries, there are seventeen gravestones in Pleasant Hill engraved with the year 1927. Two are townspeople killed in Kehoe's truck explosion, and the others are children ranging in age from seven to fourteen.

• • •

In 1953, an elementary building was constructed across Webster Road to the rear of the school. Nine years later the high school moved into a new building north of the elementary, leaving only the junior high in the old school.

Richard was serving on the school board when it was determined that the Couzens building had become obsolete — and unsafe.

During the next school year, the junior high moved in

with the high school. Our oldest, Steven, ninth grade, went to classes from seven until noon, and Tim, eighth grade, went in the afternoon. Lisa, in elementary school, wasn't affected.

With the stress and complications placed on students and parents, teachers and staff, the second bond issued passed, and our children graduated from a new high school.

• • •

Ironically the gigantic wrecking ball began its demolition at the north end of the James Couzens building, the location of the explosion forty-eight years before. The razed site was redeveloped as the James Couzens Memorial Park. At the center is the original Bath Consolidated School's cupola, which survived the disaster and remained on the reconstructed building. A Michigan historical marker, a bronze plaque bearing the names of the victims, was later installed in the park.

• • •

There were no ceremonies for the class of 1927. The graduates were simply given their diplomas without any formal recognition.

On the fiftieth anniversary of the disaster, the members of that class were invited to go through graduation with the class of 1977. Of fifteen, ten were living and nine were able to participate.

At a school reunion in 2009, I introduced myself to Irene Babcock Dunham, one hundred one at the time. I told her that our son Tim was a member of the class of 1977. She replied with a gracious smile, "Oh, it was so nice of those young people to let us graduate with them."

137

*Left to right: The class of 1927, our son Tim's graduation photo, Irene Bab-
cock Dunham and me at a school reunion*

• • •

The following are excerpts from a poem entitled "The
Last Bell" written by Mrs. W.H. Blount, Hillman, Michigan,
published May 25, 1939:

*"Mother, there's the school bell ringing, I believe
our clock is slow."*
*And the mother sighed and answered, "Yes, it's
time for you to go."*
*Up the steps, soon all are seated. One, to teacher
posies bring,*
*When a little hand is lifted, "Teacher, won't you
let us sing?"*
*And the teacher smiled and nodded, "What will
your selection be?"*
*"Oh, it's 'Jewels in the Knapsack', and it's on page
fifty-three."*
*"'When He cometh' sang the children, and the
teacher looking down*
*On their happy upturned faces, wreathed in locks
of gold and brown,*
Or the one whose flaxen ringlets 'gainst the mid-

night tresses shone,
Thought, "What jewels for a Savior, they His
loved ones and His own."
"Like the stars," the chorus swelling, laughing fac-
es, not one frown;
They shall shine in saint-like beauty, dazzling
bright gems for His crown.
"He will gather" white robed angels bore them on
their wings of love,
To the Father, who was waiting in the Blessed
Home above.
Forty children and their teachers knelt before the
Saviour King,
In His loving arms He clasped them as the Last
Bell ceased to ring.

Rationing poster

Chapter Twelve-
WORLD WAR II

"Mom, Mrs. Force didn't come to school today. Buzzy's mother, Mrs. O'Beirne, was our substitute. She said Mrs. Force isn't coming back until after Christmas vacation. She'll miss our Christmas program."

"Dawn, is Mrs. Force sick? What did Mrs. O'Beirne say about her?"

"She said her husband is fighting in the South Pacific, and she's so worried about him. Mom, where is the South Pacific? Why is she so worried?"

• • •

I loved Florence Force — all of her students did. We didn't understand much about the war except that anything that caused our teacher to miss school had to be horrible. This was the first time in my short life that I had personally felt affected by what was going on across that great ocean.

• • •

My parents were celebrating their fifth wedding anniversary on September 1, 1939, and I was two years old when the Third Reich invaded Poland. I was four when Japan attacked Pearl Harbor, and as a young child, wartime was all I ever knew.

In 1941, the United States was just coming out of the Great Depression. People were looking forward to better times after a decade of despair. But the war meant more hardships "for the duration" — however long it would take for victory.

During wartime the military fights on the frontlines. Throughout World War II it was necessary for Americans to fight on the home front. The nation was called, and Americans responded. In that process the government enlisted a catch phrase that was used in the 1930s: "Use it up, wear it out, and make it do, or do without."

America had always been a land of abundance, even in the depths of the Depression. Food was available if one could afford it, but as soon as we entered the war, shortages began.

Sugar was the first item to be rationed. The war with Japan had cut off imports from the Philippines, and cargo ships from Hawaii were diverted to the military. In order to prevent hoarding and skyrocketing prices, the Office of Price Administration (OPA) issued War Ration Book One. Distribution centers were located at local schools and staffed primarily with volunteers. Each family member received one book, and sugar could only be purchased legally with these stamps. Even then it wasn't always available at local grocery stores. Especially during canning season, women lined up early in the morning when a new shipment was expected.

By March of 1943, coffee, meat, milk, cheese, butter, oils and fats, eggs, canned fish, canned milk, and other canned and prepared foods were added to the list of rationed provisions.

Every American was entitled to a series of war ration books filled with stamps that could be used to buy restricted items, and within weeks of the first issuance, more than ninety-one percent of the U.S. population had registered to receive them. The OPA allotted a certain number of points to each food item based on its availability, and customers were allowed to use forty-eight 'blue points' to buy canned, bottled or dried foods, and sixty-four 'red points' to buy meat, fish and dairy each month — that is, if the items were in stock at the supermarket. Due to changes in the supply and demand of various goods, the OPA periodically adjusted point values, which often further complicated an already complex system that required homemakers to plan well in advance.

Victory Garden poster

Victory Gardens were another way people supported the war effort. Planting a Victory Garden was not only necessary during a time of food rationing, but was patriotic as well. Vast supplies of food were necessary for the military. Citizens were encouraged to grow and preserve as much of their own food as possible. City dwellers planted vegetables in flower beds, back yards, and even on roof tops. Empty lots were turned into neighborhood cooperatives, and government and businesses urged people to make food production a family and community effort.

Many schools planted Victory Gardens on their grounds and used their produce in school lunches. School children were recruited during late winter and early spring to help in the effort. Teachers handed out packages of Victory Garden seeds and encouraged the children to sell them to their parents, relatives, and neighbors. It was a proud moment when the money was turned in, and the children were congratulated for helping win that terrible war across the ocean.

Government and state Agricultural Extension Services printed pamphlets on growing and preserving garden produce as well as monthly meal planning guides with daily menus and recipes. Women's magazines joined the effort, and the sale of pressure canners skyrocketed.

At their peak, there were more than twenty million Victory Gardens responsible for producing forty percent of all vegetables grown in this country.

• • •

Farmers fared much better than city dwellers because we could put in huge gardens. Our basement shelves were lined with Mason jars of vegetables and fruit that Mom canned with little or no sugar.

We raised chickens for eggs and Sunday dinner. Mom put up beef and one fateful day the lid of a jar just out the pressure canner blew off. Thankfully no one was hurt, but the kitchen was a disaster with chunks of meat and broth dripping from the ceiling. We were relieved when Ewing's Grocery put in a large walk-in freezer with locker space to rent.

Our Michigan basement with its low ceiling, dirt floor, and stone walls kept potatoes, winter squash, onions, and apples fresh throughout the winter months.

Mom pasteurized our milk and skimmed off the cream for butter. She and I sat at the kitchen table turning the handle of the butter churn and watching the cream thicken. That glass butter churn with its wooden paddles has been on top of my kitchen cupboard for a very long time.

Since oils and butter were rationed, we had to reuse fat for frying. When it was no longer good for cooking, Mom collected it in a large tin can and turned it in at Ewing's store. She was paid a small amount, and the fat was sold to rendering plants for processing into explosives.

• • •

The auto industry converted their facilities to production of tanks, aircraft, weapons, and other military supplies. Dad was building aircraft rather than automobile bodies. Companies also stopped civilian manufacturing of furniture, radios, phonographs, refrigerators, vacuum cleaners, washing machines, and sewing machines.

Scrap rubber poster

• • •

Most of the world's supply of natural rubber came from plantations in Southeast Asia that were quickly occupied by the Japanese. Factories converting to military production needed rubber, and we were asked to turn in anything that was no longer usable, like tires, raincoats, gloves, and garden hoses.

New tires became almost impossible to buy. All tires had tubes at that time, and everyone carried a tube and tire repair kit as well as a jack and air pump.

A national speed limit of thirty-five miles per hour was imposed to save tires and fuel. To receive a gasoline ration card, people had to certify a need and ownership of no more than five tires. Any additional had to be forfeited.

An "A" sticker on a car windshield was the lowest priority and entitled the car owner to three to four gallons of gasoline per week for essential activities such as shopping, attending church, and going to the doctor. "B" stickers were issued to workers in the military industry entitling them to eight gallons. "C" stickers were granted to persons deemed very essential to the war effort such as doctors, mail carriers, and railroad employees. "T" rations were for trucks and buses. Lastly, "X" stickers entitled police, firefighters, civil defense workers, and ministers to unlimited supplies.

Leonard Hiatt with his Standard Oil truck brought gasoline during the growing season and pumped it into our farm storage tank for use in our tractors. Dad had a "B" sticker for work, and we didn't drive any more than was absolutely necessary.

By late 1942, other kinds of fuel were also in short supply. The military needed huge quantities for ships, tanks, and planes. Americans were warned of the coming shortage and advised to winterize their homes.

• • •

Massive amounts of metal were required to build tanks,

ships, planes, and weapons. Anything made of metal — from chicken wire to farm equipment — was rationed. Schools and community groups across the country held scrap metal drives.

Tin was needed for electrical equipment on airplanes and other essentials. Schools also competed in bringing in the largest number of tin cans. We peeled off the labels, flattened the cans and turned them in.

Paper was used for packing weapons and equipment shipped overseas. Paper drives also became a part of the war effort.

• • •

Japan's control of Indonesia cut off the main supply of kapok, which was used for the buoyancy of life preservers. Milkweed also has white, wispy hairs attached to its seeds, and it became a suitable substitute for kapok. Since milkweed is a wild plant, collection of its pods was assigned to the nation's children. Jack and I walked along fence rows and anywhere else on the farm where weeds grew. We even had organized periods during school hours to gather pods along rural roads and the railroad right of way.

• • •

Clothing and shoe factories were converted to the production of uniforms, shoes, boots, and other items for the military. The practice of using printed flour and feed sacks begun during the Great Depression increased during the war years. These sacks were used for women's and children's clothes, diapers, pillow cases, curtains, tablecloths, quilts, and other items.

Mom and I always went with Dad to the feed store. It was so exciting to look at the new offerings and choose prints for our next dresses, skirts, and aprons. I don't remember Mom ever making any clothing for Dad and Jack, but she mended pants and shirts and darned socks. Our annual trip to R&H Shoe Store in Lansing was a big occasion.

• • •

By the end of the war, the United States had more than sixteen million men and women in the armed forces with over seventy percent serving abroad. In excess of four times that many workers supported them on the home front. A multitude of new jobs were created to manufacture the tools of war, and American women rose to the occasion. Rosie the Riveter campaigns stressed the need for women to enter the work force — and they did in huge numbers.

By 1945, more than two million women were working in factories and shipyards, proving that

Rosie, the Riveter poster

they could be trained to do the same industrial work as men. They were motivated not only by patriotism and the desire for high wages but by the sense of community gained from participation in a huge undertaking. Without them, the work-force could never have produced the military supplies need-ed to win the war.

My mother-in-law, Mary Rose Hawks, worked in am-munition manufacturing at the Wolf Creek Ordnance Plant in Milan, Tennessee. She carpooled thirty miles to Milan and sometimes boarded there during the week while the children stayed with their grandparents.

On December 3, 1942, she received the Army-Navy "E" Award in recognition "of outstanding effort in the production of materials vital to the successful conduct of the war."

When the war ended, so did the military careers of millions of men. Women were then urged to resume their former lower-paying positions or return to full-time homemaking and raising children. By the end of the 1940s, thirty million babies had been born, ushering in the age of the Baby Boomers.

The seed was planted during the war for the feasibility of paid employment for women outside the home. The recruits of Rosie the Riveter opened the door for succeeding generations to enter the work force in roles traditionally reserved for men.

• • •

In order to mobilize the home front in financing the war, the Treasury Department turned to ordinary Americans whose annual median income averaged about two thousand dollars a year.

War Bonds were an investment in our country—and in our financial future. A Series E bond cost eighteen dollars and twenty-five cents and was redeemable ten years later for twenty five dollars. War savings stamps were introduced in small denominations: ten, twenty-five, and fifty cents and one and five dollars so that any citizen could support the war effort with as little as a dime. These stamps were pasted in collection booklets to be redeemed for Series E bonds.

The bond campaign was unique in that both government and private companies participated, and massive advertising campaigns used an array of media. Posters picturing Uncle Sam or a soldier on the battlefield implored people to do their part. Celebrities traveled the country, putting on parades, live shows, and radio broadcasts.

Movie theatres ended their films with the following announcement: "Fifteen thousand theatres are now selling war bonds and stamps. Buy yours today."

"Schools at War" competitions encouraged children to bring in nickels, dimes, and quarters to out-raise other schools. Even Superman, Batman, Bugs Bunny, and other cartoon characters got into the spirit reminding young people that "We're all in this together."

War bonds poster

By the end of the war, the last proceeds from the Victory War Bond campaign were deposited into the United States Treasury. More that eighty-five million Americans—half of the population—had purchased bonds totaling one hundred eighty-six billion dollars.

• • •

We were sitting in our classroom on May 8, 1945, when news of Nazi Germany's unconditional surrender reached our ears. VE Day—Victory in Europe! As the announcement came over the loudspeaker, our classroom erupted in cheers, and Mrs. Force was overcome with emotion. But the war in the Pacific waged on, and Frank Force was still in the midst of it.

• • •

On May 30, 2010, I was able to locate a phone number in Durham, North Carolina for Frank and Florence Force. I explained to Mr. Force that his wife was my teacher during the last year of the war. When I asked if I might speak with her, he told me that she had passed away ten years earlier at age seventy-eight.

I mentioned that Mrs. Force had been so worried about him during the winter of 1944 and spring of 1945 that she had missed several days of school. Mr. Force explained that he was in the Navy and had fought in six different theaters in the Pacific, mainly the Philippines and Borneo.

• • •

At the same time that the Japanese bombed Pearl Harbor, they destroyed almost half of the American aircraft in the Philippines, then a United States territory. Japanese troops soon overran the islands, and General Douglas MacArthur defensively pulled his forces back to the Bataan Peninsula. By January 1942, Manila, the capital, had fallen to the Japanese.

The outlook for control of the islands grew dimmer by the day. Fearing the capture of MacArthur, President Franklin Roosevelt ordered him to Australia to assume command of Allied forces in the Southwestern Pacific. For his valiant defense of the Philippines, the general was awarded the Congressional Medal of Honor.

MacArthur was deeply disappointed when he learned that there were far fewer Allied troops in Australia than he had hoped. He issued a statement to the press promising his men and the people of the Philippines, "I shall return." He would repeat this promise often during the next two and a half years. Left behind were ninety thousand American and Filipino troops who lacked food, supplies, and support and were soon captured.

Bataan fell in April, and seventy thousand American and Filipino troops were forced to undertake what became known as the infamous Bataan Death March. At least seven thousand died, and the next month when Corregidor surrendered, fifteen thousand more were captured. With limited troops and weapons of war, the Joint Chiefs of Staff had no immediate plans for their liberation.

• • •

General Douglas MacArthur leading the invasion of the Philippines

In July 1944, President Roosevelt met with his two Pacific Theater commanders, General MacArthur and Admiral Chester Nimitz. MacArthur insisted that the next move in the Pacific must be the liberation of the Philippines. Japan would be cut off from Indonesian oil, and the islands would provide a place from which the final assaults on the Japanese homeland could be launched.

On October 20, one hundred thirty-two thousand troops of the Sixth Army landed on the Island of Leyte. MacArthur waded ashore a few hours later accompanied by members of the Philippine government and press. That day he made a radio broadcast in which he announced, "People of the Philippines, I have returned! By the grace of Almighty God, our forces stand again on Philippine soil."

Only one third of the men MacArthur had left behind on March 11, 1942, survived to see his return. "I'm a little late," he told them, "but we finally came."

• • •

Frank Force, aboard the LST-709, a Navy amphibious tank-landing ship, participated in the Leyte landings beginning on November 10, and the island was taken on December 26. It was during these fierce battles that Mrs. Force missed school and prayed for her husband. Those of us from praying families joined her.

• • •

The campaign for Leyte proved the first and most decisive operation in the American campaign of liberating the Philippines. With more than two hundred fifty thousand Japanese controlling the other islands, fierce fighting loomed ahead.

Frank Force's ship continued in the battles for the southern Philippines, landing troops and tanks on Palawan Island in January 1945 and the Visayan Islands in March and April. The

The Sixth Army landing on Leyte

LST-709 continued in the assault and occupation of the Oki-nawa Guinto and the Brunei Bay operations in June earning two battle stars for meritorious service.

• • •

Even though Germany had unconditionally surrendered on May 8, 1945, Japan refused the terms of the Potsdam Dec-laration, the statement calling for the surrender of all Japa-nese troops. To prevent an invasion of the Japanese mainland in which untold thousands of our military—as well as Japa-nese—would die, the decision was made to drop an atomic bomb on Hiroshima on August 6. The Japanese High Com-mand still refused to surrender, and another bomb decimated the city of Nagasaki on August 9.

• • •

Whenever Dad was in the barn, we could hear the radio. We listened to Detroit Tiger baseball—and the news. At seven o'clock on the evening of August 15, 1945, we had just fin-ished milking when it was announced that President Harry S. Truman was about to hold a press conference.

A war-weary nation waited in breathless anticipation as our president proclaimed that the Japanese had finally agreed to an unconditional surrender. VJ Day—Victory in Japan! Af-ter almost six long years, it was finally over.

On that summer evening we hugged and cheered. I was only eight, and war was all I had ever known. But I could sense that something amazing, marvelous, and way beyond my childish comprehension had just occurred that would transform our world and give us hope again.

• • •

Francis LeClear, a member of our church, survived the

Bataan Death March. He married, moved to Bath, taught at Lansing Community College, and raised six children. His two youngest, Jimmy and Mark, were high school and college friends of our son Tim. Fran didn't talk about the war.

• • •

Mrs. Force taught one more year at Bath. By then her husband had returned from the military, and they could get on with their lives.

Recently, I went online again and learned that Frank Force had passed away on February 21, 2015, at age ninety-five. I was able to pull up his obituary and learn some additional information.

Frank and Florence met during their first semester at Central Michigan University and married two years later. After graduating in 1943, he joined the Navy.

After the war, Frank graduated from the University of Michigan Law School, clerked with the Michigan Supreme Court, and took a position with REO Motor Car Company in Lansing. In 1959, he became the first attorney for the Ford Motor Credit Company and finished his career there, retiring as vice president in 1979.

Frank and Florence moved to Southern Pines, North Carolina. They traveled extensively, and Frank pursued his passion for golf. After Florence passed away in 2000, he moved to Durham to be closer to his children.

Frank Force was a man of honor and integrity. A devoted family man, he served not only his family and country but lived out his years serving his local church and his community.

PFC Ralph TerBeek, 372nd Army Corp of Engineers

Chapter Thirteen -
RALPH TERBEEK

"We've been prisoners in this barn for five days. Our guys are coming soon, and these Krauts have got to get out. What are they going to do with us?"

"Shush. Listen."

"Brennen sie die scheune. Sie Amerikaner sind kommenden."

"Ralph, you know Dutch and you can understand German. What's he saying?"

"He said, 'Burn the barn. The Americans will be coming.'"

"Burn the barn? They're going to burn us?"

"Quiet! His men are arguing with him."

"Kapitän, sie können nicht ermorden. Sie sind Gefangene des Krieges.

"What was that?"

"They told the captain he can't kill us—we're prisoners of war. They're still arguing. All you guys in touch with God, start praying!"

• • •

Ralph TerBeek was born April 13, 1922, in Byron Center, Michigan. He grew up on the family farm near Beaver Dam, a tiny rural community consisting of the Christian Reformed Church and School and Heizer's General Store. Ralph and his three younger siblings attended the church school.

Farm families as well as the rest of the nation were hugely affected by the Great Depression. During the four years following Black Tuesday, the average income of small family farms fell to less than one third of the 1929 level.

Two-percent interest on the mortgage was more than the TerBeeks could manage. To make matters worse, Mrs. TerBeek lost two babies during those terrible days, and the medical bills mounted. Bank foreclosure forced the family to lose their farm, home, and livelihood. They moved to Plainwell and rented a farm across the road from Ralph's grandparents. He worked on both farms through his junior high years.

At the end of eighth grade, Mr. TerBeek took Ralph aside and told him that he wouldn't be going on to high school. Times were hard and as the eldest son, he was needed to work on the farms. Greatly disappointed, Ralph accepted the fact that there was no other way for his parents, siblings, and grandparents to survive without his labors.

Economic times improved and when Ralph was sixteen, the family moved to a small farm near the village of Moline. Ralph was hired at the Bissell Company making carpet sweepers and worked there for a year and a half. The family attended Moline Christian Reformed Church, and Ralph and his second cousin Pete Raad were in the youth group together.

• • •

After Pearl Harbor more than ten million men were drafted to serve in the military. Ralph and Pete received their notices, and on a cold day in January 1942, they traveled to Port Sheridan, Indiana for induction into the United States Army. Ralph accepted his duty to serve his country with the same devotion he had served his family.

From Port Sheridan, Ralph and Pete were sent to Camp Claiborne, Louisiana to receive basic training and artillery practice. Besides the rigors of military training, they had to endure the climate of Louisiana. It was either hot and dusty or rainy and humid.

Ralph and Pete were assigned to the Army Corp of Engineers, whose primary mission was to keep the Allied armies moving. Training concentrated on demolition, bridge and road construction, and combat.

In August 1943, Ralph and Pete were among the first American troops to arrive in South Wales. They were stationed at the British Army base, Island Farm, and assigned to build field hospitals.

The American GIs were well received by the community of Bridigend. Ralph, Pete, and two other buddies began attending the Baptist Chapel where they met Mr. and Mrs. Arthur Davies and their teenage daughter, June. The Davies often invited Ralph and Pete and their buddies to tea after church, and their home was always open whenever the young men had time off.

In December, Ralph had a thirty-day pass, and Arthur Davies took him on a sightseeing tour of London. It was a very memorable experience for Ralph, not only for what he saw and photographed, but for the great kindness this English gentleman showed to his young American friend.

After leaving South Wales, Ralph's division, the 372nd

Army Corp of Engineers, was ordered to Purflete, a very small town eight miles south of London. The British camp was old, and the GIs lived in pup tents.

In advance of the invasion of France, the English Channel had to be prepared for the crossing of Allied forces. American troops worked with the British military and civilians to build floating dry docks. They also constructed fifteen thousand-ton barges that were sunk off Utah and Omaha Beaches for unloading troops and supplies.

As the war progressed, thousands of German soldiers were captured or surrendered, and Island Farm was transformed into a prisoner-of-war camp. By the end of the war, almost two thousand prisoners were held there.

Many German troops had been forced into the Army of the Third Reich as it swarmed across Europe. These men hated the Nazis and readily surrendered to American and British forces. The early prisoners were mainly "other ranks," cooperative and willing to perform duties in the camp. They were relieved to be out of the front lines and thankful for the hope of living through the war.

The prisoners with the lowest security clearance were allowed to leave the camp at certain times. On Sundays a few went to the Baptist Chapel, and the Davies welcomed them into their hearts and home just as they had the Americans.

Heinz Brauniger was eighteen when he was drafted, handed a rifle, and forced to the front lines. Within a few weeks he was in a position to surrender to Allied troops and was taken to Island Camp. Heinz met the Davies family at church and was one of their frequent visitors. He and June began spending time together, and a romance blossomed. With his release at the end of the war, Heinz and June married and remained in South Wales. Heinz and another prisoner of war married to an English girl opened a women's clothing store. Heinz and June were blessed with a daughter, and they celebrated their fiftieth wedding anniversary before his death.

• • •

In June 1944, the German army began using a very unique and deadly weapon called the "Vengeance One." Better known as "Buzz Bombs," these rockets made a very distinct sound as they flew overhead at low altitude. When the timing mechanism expired, they fell to earth and exploded. The military, as well as Londoners, learned to go about their normal business as these huge twenty-five-foot cross-shaped rockets flew overhead. Once people heard the engine cut off, they had to take immediate cover. Ralph shuddered as he relived those dreadful days and long nights more than sixty-five years before. But the worst was yet to come.

• • •

On D-Day, June 6, 1944, over one hundred sixty thousand Allied troops and thirty thousand vehicles landed along a fif-

Normandy landing

ty-mile stretch of the German occupied French coastline. Omaha Beach, one of five sectors of the Normandy landings, was the longest of the landing areas with the toughest defenses. The water and beach were littered with mines, and the entire beach was overlooked by one-hundred-foot cliffs staffed with German infantry. The first assault experienced the worst ordeal of the D-Day operation. Aided by heavy naval bombardment, Allied troops crossed the beach and began scaling the cliffs. Paratroopers closed in on the German defenses from behind, enabling the beach exits to be secured by midday.

All but two of twenty-nine amphibious tanks were destroyed, and almost all of the senior officers were killed or wounded. Despite a fifty-percent casualty rate, the survivors regrouped and pressed on. Americans suffered two thousand four hundred casualties that day, but by nightfall thirty-four thousand troops had landed.

In July 1944, thirty days after the invasion, the 372nd landed on Omaha Beach. They moved a mile inland and set up camp in an open field surrounded by hedgerows. The rain and mud made for deplorable conditions as they continued their advance further into France. The next month, after four years of German occupation, the Allies liberated Paris with the help of French resistance troops led by General Charles de Gaulle.

• • •

The 372nd went on to Belgium where they served as support troops for American, British, and French forces. They built stockades for German prisoners and moved behind enemy lines securing towns and villages.

In one city Ralph's outfit moved into a Catholic Church. Ralph was assigned as an electrician's helper, and changing the voltage was time-consuming as they converted the gymnasium into a field hospital. The air was alive with German dive bombers constantly attacking the ground forces. The troops just tried to do their job and survive.

After Belgium was secured, they moved into Luxembourg. The 372nd wasn't a combat company, but they followed the front line troops to maintain supply lines. On one occasion they stopped to get their bearings after traveling all night. Even without field glasses, they spotted Nazis on the other side of a river. Ralph and the other men moved back quickly and quietly.

• • •

Ralph had been looking forward to two weeks of rest and relaxation in a camp in France. After the horrors of war, this was supposed to be a pleasant time. Instead, it proved to be extremely devastating.

For about a year before being drafted, Ralph had dated Gertrude Door, a girl from Grand Rapids and cousin of his brother's girlfriend. They fell in love and became engaged.

Gertrude promised to wait for Ralph, and pleasant thoughts of her and their coming marriage encouraged him through rough times.

Ralph had detected nothing out of the ordinary in her earlier correspondence, and the "Dear John" letter came as a complete surprise. Gertrude explained that she felt called to be a missionary, and she could better serve God as a single woman. She was sorry—that was all.

Ralph was deeply hurt. How could Gertrude do this to him? She had promised to wait. She had promised to marry him. But Ralph had to go on and put personal feelings aside. There was a war to fight—and win.

• • •

The 372nd had been trained as combat as well as support troops, and the men were sent to join General George S. Patton's Third Army. Ralph described Patton as "'Old blood and

163

guts.' He carried two pearl-handled pistols and cussed a blue streak. 'Give 'em hell, boys, give 'em hell!' He was a rough sucker, a demanding sort of a guy. He had no pity even for his own troops."

When the Third Army approached Frankfort, General Patton stated that any resistance would be a signal to call in Allied bombers. Sniper fire erupted, and Patton ordered the attack. Incendiary bombs rained down, setting fire to everything in their paths. Within seven minutes the city was leveled. The 372nd entered to rebuild the railroad tracks and train stations.

• • •

Hitler sent a quarter million troops across an eighty-five mile stretch of the Allied front from southern Belgium into Luxembourg. German troops advanced some fifty miles into Allied lines creating a deadly "bulge." On December 16, 1944, the Battle of the Bulge began. The 372nd was on the front lines in Luxembourg on Christmas Eve. Ralph and the other troops shivered miserably in foxholes as the temperature dropped to twelve below zero.

One evening while on patrol, Ralph and about twenty troops were surprised by German soldiers. With guns pointed directly at them, there was no choice but to surrender. For five days they were held in the barn of an abandoned farm. Allied forces were advancing, and the Germans knew they had to retreat back to their lines. They had to make a decision about what to do with these enemy combatants.

The Captain shouted, "Burn the barn! When the Americans come through here, they'll know they are fighting the Army of the Third Reich!"

Because Ralph grew up in a Dutch-speaking home, he could understand enough to know what was being said. He explained the situation to the other men, and fervent prayers for divine intervention went up to the God of heaven.

The sergeant spoke up. "Captain, you can't burn these men. They're our enemies, but they've surrendered. They're prisoners of war." Others joined the sergeant. After a heated argument the captain gave in, and they quickly left. Ralph and the others beat on the door, and it finally gave way. Shortly afterward the Allies moved in and the men were reunited with their forces.

• • •

He that dwelleth in the secret place of the most High shall abide
under the shadow of the Almighty. I will say of the LORD, 'He is
my refuge and my fortress, my God, in Him will I trust. . .' For he
shall give his angels charge over thee, to keep thee in all thy ways. . .
Because he hath set his love upon me, therefore will I deliver him:
I will set him on high because he hath known my name. He shall
call upon me, and I will answer him; I will be with him in trouble;
I will deliver him and honor him. With long life will I satisfy him
and show him my salvation –Psalm 91 (KJV)

• • •

General Patton's expertise in tank command helped frustrate the December 1944 counter-offensive in the Battle of the Bulge. Under his command the Third Army swept into Germany and Czechoslovakia. By the end of January 1945, the battle was over, but more than seventy-six thousand Americans had been killed, wounded, or captured. The Allies regained the territory that they had previously held.

In March, United States forces crossed the Rhine River, and the Germans retreated back to Germany. The following month, as Soviet forces pushed into Berlin, Adolf Hitler took shelter in his bomb-proof bunker in Berlin. He married his mistress Eva Braun before poisoning her and shooting himself. On May 7, 1945, General Dwight Eisenhower accepted Germany's unconditional surrender at Reims, France.

• • •

After more reconstruction in Germany and France, the men of the 372nd arrived in New York City on July 2, 1945 for a thirty-day furlough. They were then assigned to duty in the United States Postal Service in Queens. Undelivered letters written to the thousands killed in the war had to be sent back to their families. Five GIs were required for the work that two postal employees usually did in normal times. After two depressing months the men were called back to the Engineer Replacement Training Center headquarters at Fort Belvoir, Virginia for further training. The war in the Pacific was still raging.

The 372nd was preparing to board a troop ship for the invasion of the mainland when the Japanese High Command officially surrendered on August 15. World War II had finally ended.

The men were discharged at Fort Dix, New Jersey, on October 18. Ralph had served forty-six months and earned the European-African-Middle Eastern Campaign Service Medal and the Good Conduct Medal.

. . .

The Moline Christian Reformed Church sent out the *Moline Echoes,* a monthly newsletter to all of the forty-four servicemen in its congregation. It contained hometown events and an inspiring message from the pastor.

Sarah Moore was a member of the Berean Church, but she attended the youth group at Moline. Sarah became friends with the other girls who were publishing the paper and joined them.

Ralph was at a friend's house one evening looking through the 1944 Moline High School yearbook. He came across Sarah Moore's picture and said, "Who the dickens is she?"

Sarah worked in the general store in Moline and took turned-in ration stamps to the bank every day. Angie De-Haan, a young woman who worked in the bank, was married to Ralph's cousin Carl. One afternoon Angie said to Sarah, "Ralph TerBeek is home from the service. Why don't you two get together?"

On a Sunday evening Ralph decided to look up this young woman Angie was always talking about. Ralph's brother Tony was dating a girl from Kalamazoo. She had come for the day and needed a ride home. Tony asked, "Ralph, why don't you call up Sarah and invite her to ride with us." Sarah was helping with her ailing grandmother that evening, but her aunt offered to stay with her. Ralph and Sarah had a pleasant evening getting to know one another.

When Angie heard about it, she was thrilled. "Sarah, why don't you two get together so we can be relatives forever?"

Six months later, Ralph and Sarah were engaged. They were married on October 18, 1946, a year to the day after Ralph received his discharge. They were blessed with four children and celebrated more than sixty-two years of marriage before Sarah's death.

• • •

Gertrude Door never married. She was very active in her Grand Rapids church and supported herself by teaching piano. Ralph saw her once at a wedding of mutual friends, and they said "Hi" to one another.

• • •

In 1978, Ralph and Sarah took a two-week trip to South Wales and stayed with Heinz and June. Sadly Arthur Davies had passed away, but they visited at length with Mrs. Davies. She admitted that the family had used part of their weekly ration stamps to provide a Sunday meal for the young Americans so far from home.

Visiting South Wales was very special for Ralph and Sarah. It gave him the opportunity to share many memories — an unforgettable time in his life.

• • •

At age ninety-four, Ralph is in poor health and resides in an assisted living facility. He longs for the day when he can join his Lord and his wife in heaven.

Ralph TerBeek is a proud member of the Greatest Generation.

Ralph and Sarah TerBeek

Dawn Voorheis Hawks

World War II poster

Chapter Fourteen-
MEN OF MOLINE

"Dawn, I want to thank you for writing my story. I've given copies of it to all my family and friends at church—even my pastor."

"Ralph, it was my privilege. A story such as yours needed to be told."

"Did I tell you that there were forty-four of us from the Moline Christian Reformed Church who served in the military? Many years after the war, our accounts were compiled in Memories of World War II Veterans. Here's my copy. Would you like to write some of these experiences in your memoirs?"

"Yes, Ralph, I certainly would. How many of the forty-four survived?"

"Forty-three of us returned—but only by the grace of God."

• • •

The following are excerpts from *Memories of World War II Veterans*.

From the account of Gerald W. VanDenBerg, Private First Class, United States Army. Inducted in August 1944.

President Roosevelt presented radio chats to the nation. 'I hate war.' We farm boys agreed with the president. We hated war too, but we were in the army. I was twenty years old, and I had never traveled more than twenty miles from Moline. The troop train from Detroit took us to Camp Wolters, Texas. This was my first train ride, and I was fourteen hundred miles from home.

After sixteen weeks of training, each of us would replace a casualty somewhere. Fighting was fierce in Europe. On December 16, 1944, Hitler tried to split the Allied armies by a surprise thrust from Belgium through Luxembourg. By Christmas thirty German divisions had opened a bulge fifty miles deep into the Allied lines. Our troops were caught off guard and outnumbered ten to one. We suffered the biggest mass surrender of American soldiers since Bataan—some four thousand in one day.

Would I be fighting with General George Patton in the Battle of the Bulge? Sixteen weeks would have brought me to Christmas Day. That battle was fought during December and January. We suffered the largest number of casualties in any battle of our history, seventy-five thousand dead and wounded.

History is written by the finger of God, and we only know the now. Why did I get sick during those first weeks of training? A few days in the hospital meant a delay so that my training ended in February 1945. By then our forces had taken back the ground they had lost.

Our troop train took us quickly across Europe: England, France, the Netherlands, and Muenster, Germany. I was under the command of Patton's Third Army. I had my steel helmet and an M1 rifle with live ammunition. Was I ready to kill German soldiers?

The Allied Forces bombed Berlin day and night. I can still hear the roar of the bombers. The army organized training exercises at Muenster before we went to the front lines. I was wounded two months later, April 29, and admitted to the field hospital on the front lines—a large tent with a Red Cross. While I was there, the war in Europe ended.

With my buddies headed to the Japanese mainland, I was flown with the other wounded to Paris. For me the war was over. 'You are my God; my times are in your hands.

• • •

From the account of Staff Sergeant Donald Haveman. Entered the Army in September, 1942.

A few months later I received a telegram from my wife stating that we had been blessed with a baby girl. I did not see her for two and a half years.

The 123rd fought the Japanese in Dutch New Guinea. In January 1945, we were sent to the island of Luzon, where we took the summer capital of the Philippines. It was during this battle that I knew the Lord was watching over me.

A mortar shell exploded so close that it blew me off my feet and hit five other men right near me. I can only say that God was with me all the way, as men fell by my side, never to return to their loved ones. I offer to God my thanks, honor, glory, and praise.

• • •

From the account of Ellert Hendriksman, First Lieutenant, United States Army. Arrived in Italy late 1942 and was assigned to the Third Battalion as a platoon leader.

We reached our outfit just before dawn and were sent out on patrol. Three hours later we should have been taken prisoner. Five Jerrys came up behind us, but they wanted to be our prisoners, as the war would then be over for them. We took them back and had to go on a patrol ahead.

After about two hours we came to a minefield. Calling the mine detector squad, we went through it to protect the men who were under small-arms fire. Coming back through to check how the mine squad was doing, one went off. I was twenty-five yards away, but I still received thirty wounds. After about two years in and out of hospitals, I was discharged in October 1946.

• • •

From the account of Christian VandenBerg, United States Naval Reserve. Entered the service in May 1944, and took basic training at Great Lakes, Illinois.

After a short stay in San Francisco, I got on a troop ship and headed for the South Pacific, where we were replacements for those who had been killed. I participated in air strikes on Saipan, Iwo Jima, the Philippines, Okinawa, Formosa, and the Leyte Islands.

On the night of November 3, we were torpedoed by a Japanese submarine and told to abandon ship. We were picked up by a destroyer and transferred to an aircraft carrier. Forty-six men died. A few times I came close to death, but the Lord spared me.

May we be grateful for each day given us, thankful for sins forgiven, and when death approaches, look forward to eternal life.

• • •

From the account of Arnold Potts, United States Marine Corps. Shipped to the South Pacific in 1944.

We were aboard ship on our way to combat. After a few days we were in enemy territory. There were sixteen ships in our convoy, and we were aboard for fifty-two days before seeing land.

Soon about three hundred fifty ships appeared: aircraft carriers, battleships, cruisers, and troopships. Before daybreak the next morning, the beach was aglow with fire from warships and planes dropping bombs. When the dust settled, it was our turn. Hundreds of landing craft with tanks and riflemen hit the beach.

The island of Guam is part volcanic and coral rock. Many natural caves and tunnels were ideal hiding places for the enemy. With little food and sleep, we slowly advanced.

On the seventh day my leg was injured, and I was ordered to go to the makeshift field hospital. On the way I encountered sniper fire. Suddenly, a large shell exploded about twenty feet ahead leaving me temporarily unconscious. Later I crawled to an enemy foxhole and recovered enough to reach the medics. I was grateful to

God for deliverance. I spent four months in hospitals.

I do not regret my time in the military. There were high points we enjoyed and there were low points that will never be voiced or repeated. Thank God for peace and freedom!

• • •

From the account of Cornelius Potts, United States Army Band, aboard a ship bound for New Guinea in February 1944.

The region was jungle and very steamy hot. Our duties were to guard an airstrip on the island of Halmohara.

The Japs had an air strip about fifty miles away, and just about every night we had air raids and slept in foxholes. I saw dog fights and many planes shot down — and we lost men. If ever I prayed, it was here. I thanked God for His protecting care and for parents and church who taught me to pray.

We left in March 1945 for the island of Luzon in the Philippines. There were many caves with Japs inside. Refusing to surrender, many were buried alive by armored bulldozers that closed up the caves. The stench of death was everywhere.

After the area was secured, we traveled down to the lowland and trained for the invasion of Japan. In August, we were watching a movie one night, and the speaker suddenly cut off. The company commander told us Japan had surrendered. All went wild — shouting, hugging, you name it. We were shipped to the city of Kobe, Japan for occupation.

I was discharged in November 1945. It was a thrill to

hold my little two-year-old girl that I had never seen. Above all, thanks to God who brought me and my three brothers all safely home.

• • •

From the account of Edward Potts, Sergeant, United States Army. Left New York in 1943 with seven ships and two destroyer escorts.

Three days from England our ship collided with a fuel tanker. Fuel was floating all around us, and fortunately, no fire erupted. The damage to our ship was high enough above the water line that we could slowly continue on to England. By the grace of God, it didn't blow up or sink although two lives were lost.

From England we went to France and then on to Germany. The Nazis had stopped fighting by that time, and we never had to fire our guns.

I met a Dachau concentration camp prisoner who had been freed a short time before. He took me through the camp and explained everything that had gone on from beginning to end. The only words to explain it were 'terrible and unbelievable.'

I arrived home in March 1946. I've always felt sorry for my folks. Although our brother Herman, United States Air Force, wasn't sent overseas, it must have been very hard for them with four boys in the service at the same time.

• • •

From the account of Ralph Sytsma, Master Lance Corporal, United States Marine Corps. Inducted June, 1941.

177

In August 1944, we boarded warships and crossed the English Channel for Normandy. I was shocked when we arrived at the beach. The water was blood-red, and the beach was covered with dead. The wounded were waiting to be loaded onto ships.

As I stood there, I could see in my mind's eye the five thousand ships spewing out their troops. I could hear huge Navy guns shelling the German enforcement. I could hear the deafening noise of battle and could sense the smell of death— the chaos.

In the fall of 1944, my battalion began a six-month walk to Bastogne fighting German stragglers all the way. At one point we could only sleep in the basement of a bombed-out hotel. Ironically, German soldiers, also in need of a place to sleep, occupied the rooms upstairs. We knew they were there, and when we awoke, we confronted one another. But tired of war, tired of all the death and dying, we each went our own ways.

• • •

From the account of Robert VanDenBerg, Sergeant, United States Army. Trained and served at several state-side army camps.

On June 3, 1944, I was on a transport ship bound for Italy, assigned to the Fifth Army under the command of General Mark Clark.

We traveled by truck from Naples to headquarters near Rome. We could see the incredible devastation that war causes. It was amazing that the old city of Rome was left untouched.

The Germans were being driven northward and dug into the Apennine Mountains. The winter months were

178

extremely rough, and the fighting was fierce. We were bombarded with artillery, mortar, and sniper fire along with attacks by German planes. The German armies continued to flee up to the Austrian border where they surrendered. I am thankful that by the grace of God, I was not injured.

Our division, the Thirty-fourth Infantry, had the distinction of being not only the first to land in the European Theatre, but also to have over six hundred days in combat, more than any other. We were credited with capturing more than forty-thousand prisoners.

The Thirty-fourth ranked second to none and stands high on the scroll of honor among the greatest fighting units that ever carried the stars and stripes into battle. I returned to Moline, but the account of my friend, Al, has a much different ending.

· · ·

From the account of Albert DeVries, Sergeant, United States Army. The only serviceman from our church who didn't return from the horrors of war. Al went overseas in June 1943. He was stationed in Australia and New Guinea before taking part in the invasion of the Admiralty Islands.

On a night patrol his unit infiltrated to within forty yards of an enemy perimeter before they were discovered. The Japanese laid down a solid sheet of fire pinning the troopers to the ground. Al signaled for his unit to withdraw while he engaged the enemy. Singlehandedly he fought a delaying action. Wounded by mortar fire, he remained until all men were safe and then dragged himself back to American lines. He died a few hours later, January 1, 1945.

Al's citation read: "His devotion to his fellow men and his extreme sacrifice gained him the undying respect of all who witnessed his actions and perpetuated his name in their memories.' Al's favorite hymn was 'God is Our Refuge and Our Strength."

• • •

God is our refuge and our strength, our ever present aid,
And therefore though the earth remove, we will not be afraid.
Though hills amidst the seas be cast; though foaming waters roar,
Yes, though the mighty billows shake the mountains on the shore.
A river flows whose streams make glad the city of our God,
The holy place wherein the Lord most high has his abode.
Since God is in the midst of her, unmoved her wall shall stand
For God will be her early help when trouble is at hand.
The nations raged, the kingdoms moved, but when His voice was heard,
The troubled earth was stilled to peace before His mighty Word.
The Lord of Hosts is on our side, our safety is secure:
The God of Jacob is for us a refuge strong and sure.
O come, behold what wondrous works Jehovah's hand has wrought,
Come see what desolation great He on the earth

has brought.
To utmost ends of all the earth He causes war to
cease:
The weapons of the strong destroyed, He makes
abiding peace.
Be still and know that I am God, O'er all exalted
high;
The subject nations of the earth, My name shall
magnify.
The Lord of Host is on our side, our safety is
secure;
The God of Jacob is for us a refuge strong and sure.

Captain Mitsuo Fuchida

Chapter Fifteen
MITSUO FUCHIDA

"Dawn, did you see this article in the Grand Rapids Press? Today is the seventieth anniversary of VJ Day. World War II vets are being honored across the country."

"Seventy years ago. Not many of the vets are still alive. I'm so glad we went to Pearl Harbor. Richard, do you remember that plaque in Memorial Park about the Japanese pilot who led the attack and later became a Christian missionary?"

• • •

Mitsuo Fuchida enrolled in the Japanese Naval Academy at age eighteen. Upon graduation he joined the Naval Air Force and served as an aircraft carrier pilot for the next fifteen years. As the most experienced pilot in the Japanese Navy, he was chosen chief commander for the Pearl Harbor Mission.

A fleet of Japanese aircraft carriers and escort ships stationed two hundred miles off Oahu prepared to launch three hundred fifty fighters, bombers, and torpedo planes. The objective was to surprise and destroy the American Pacific Fleet, airfields, and aircraft. A successful mission would put Japan in position to gain control of the South Pacific.

• • •

December 7, 1941 began as a quiet Sunday morning at the Pearl Harbor Naval Base near Honolulu, Hawaii. At 7:55 a.m., fifty thousand American troops were sleeping, eating breakfast, relaxing on the sunny decks, or preparing to attend church services. On the cruiser Helena, some of the Marines were getting ready for a softball game.

• • •

Viewing the eight battleships lying peacefully below, Fuchida shouted the war cry: "Tora! Tora! Tora!" Japanese planes filled the skies over Pearl Harbor. Bombs and bullets rained onto airfields and vessels moored below.

Fifteen minutes into the mission, a huge bomb smashed through the deck of the battleship Arizona and landed in her forward ammunition magazine. The ship exploded and sank with eleven hundred men trapped inside. Torpedoes pierced the shell of the battleship Oklahoma, sinking her with four hundred aboard. The other battleships sustained significant damage. The loss of life was staggering — two thousand four hundred — and more than twelve hundred wounded.

• • •

For the next three hours, Captain Fuchida circled at a higher altitude to assess the damage. In his report to the command center, he concluded that the mission was a major success. Eighteen ships and more than three hundred planes were damaged or destroyed along with airfields and dry docks.

Fuchida was the last pilot to leave the scene. Amazingly his plane survived twenty-one large flak holes and with the frayed control cable hanging together by a single strand. An unseen hand seemed to be protecting him. By the end of the war, he was the sole survivor of the seven commanders and thirty-two squadron leaders he led at Pearl Harbor.

Mitsuo Fuchida became a national hero and was granted an audience with Emperor Hirohito. Thousands cheered and sang his praises.

• • •

The Navy's ability to reclaim the fleet was considered one of history's greatest salvage feats. Only three of the sunken warships were damaged beyond repair. The Japanese high command later came to realize that on that fateful December morning, they had won the battle but lost the war.

• • •

Six months after Pearl Harbor, the United States defeated Japan in one of the most decisive naval campaigns of World War II. On the aircraft carrier Akagi, preparing to lead the aerial battle, Fuchida was suddenly grounded for an emergency appendectomy.

The Akagi, along with three other carriers and a heavy cruiser — the entire strength of the task force — were destroyed. Fuchida's life was spared when his shipmates dragged him from the smoking ruins and put him aboard a destroyer.

With the carriers sunk, the surviving pilots had nowhere to land, and running out of fuel, they crashed into the sea. More than three hundred Japanese aircraft were destroyed.

• • •

Fuchida was in Hiroshima attending a week-long conference with Japanese army officers the day before the atom bombing. An urgent message from Navy headquarters ordered him to Tokyo. Following the bombing, he returned to Hiroshima with a party sent to assess the damage. All of those men gradually died of radiation poisoning, but Fuchida exhibited no symptoms. Why had death's sword spared him again?

• • •

Because of his military relevance, General Douglas MacArthur summoned Captain Fuchida to Tokyo to testify on behalf of a number of Japanese officers charged with war crimes. Fuchida determined to collect his own evidence to prove that the Americans were as inhuman toward Japanese captives as were his countrymen.

He met with one hundred fifty POWs returning to Japan from the United States. One, a former friend, told him that they were treated surprisingly well. He related an incredible account of an eighteen-year-old American girl who had come to the camp as a volunteer social worker.

The POWs were amazed by Margaret Covell. They called her Peggy, and she would do anything to help them within the rules of the prison. Three weeks after she arrived, a prisoner asked her, "Why are you so kind to us?"

Her answer was, "Because Japanese soldiers killed my parents." The prisoners were astonished as she told her story.

Peggy was a missionary kid, and her parents, James and Charma Covell, taught at the Kanto Gukuin School near Tokyo. They opposed Japanese aggression against neighboring countries and for their own protection the Northern Baptist Mission Board transferred them to the Philippines. Soon after, the Japanese invaded.

Many missionaries were arrested and put in prison camps. Along with nine others the Covells fled to the hills, and for two years they were hidden and protected by Filipinos. They even put together a makeshift chapel.

The day came when the Covells were discovered. The soldiers mistook their small domestic radio for a communication device, charged them as spies, and sentenced them to death.

• • •

Captain Fuchida was astonished to hear such an account, and he was filled with shame. He talked to other former POWs who had known Peggy and soon lost interest in attempting to find instances of brutality. He even searched for sources in the Philippines to verify the account of the Covells' deaths. He was told that as they knelt, blindfolded, waiting for the swish of the sword, they prayed for their captors. This concept was completely incomprehensible to Japanese rationale. How could people possibly forgive their enemies?

• • •

Peggy had no news of her parents' fate until the end of the three-year occupation. She was full of horror and hatred, but she came to realize that they would have prayed for the forgiveness and salvation of their murderers. She decided to follow their example.

• • •

In 1948, Fuchida was again ordered to testify in Tokyo, and at a train station, he was handed a pamphlet entitled, "I Was a Prisoner of Japan." The subject was Jacob DeShazer, a member of the Doolittle Raiders, who bombed Japan in 1942 in response to the attack on Pearl Harbor.

After crash landing, DeShazer was captured and imprisoned in Nanking, China. There, he witnessed the execution of three of his crewmembers while another slowly died of malnutrition. He questioned why his life was being spared. Brutality, torture, death—his violent hatred of the Japanese captors continued to escalate.

About halfway into their forty-month confinement, the prisoners were given a Bible which they all shared. When it became DeShazer's turn, he read voraciously and was greatly moved by Jesus' prayer in Luke 23:24: "Father, forgive them for they know not what they do." The dynamic power of Christ's message changed his entire attitude toward his captors. He vowed that if he were liberated, he would someday return to Japan to introduce others to this life-changing book.

• • •

For the second time, an account of the grace to forgive one's enemies rocked Fuchida. Despite his Buddhist heritage he bought a Bible and eagerly began reading. Like DeShazer he was captivated by Luke's account of Jesus' prayer.

"I was impressed that I was certainly one of those for whom he had prayed. The many men I had killed had been slaughtered in the name of patriotism, for I did not understand the love which Christ wishes to implant within every heart.

"Right at that moment, I seemed to meet Jesus for the first time. I understood the meaning of his death as a substitute for my wickedness. I requested him to forgive my sins and change me from a bitter, disillusioned ex-pilot into a well-balanced Christian. That date, April 12, 1950, I became a new person. My complete view of life was changed by the intervention of Jesus Christ. He became my personal Savior."

• • •

After the war, Jacob DeShazer attended Seattle Pacific College and planted churches in Japan. In 1950, he had just finished a forty-day fast for revival when Fuchida came to his home. DeShazer warmly welcomed him, and the men became life-long friends. They sometimes traveled together in evangelistic campaigns.

Mitsuo Fuchida attended a theological college in Tokyo, became a Presbyterian minister, and preached in his native country and throughout Asian-American communities. He and his family eventually settled in the United States.

Fuchida authored two books: *From Pearl Harbor to Calvary*, and his autobiography, *For That One Day*. He co-authored *Midway: The Battle that Doomed Japan*.

Often Fuchida stated: "I would give anything to retract my actions at Pearl Harbor, but it is impossible. Instead I now

work at striking the death blow to the basic hatred which infests the human heart and causes such tragedies. And that hatred cannot be uprooted without Jesus Christ. He is the only answer."

Captain Mitsuo Fuchida and Jacob DeShazer

Sources

Chapter One

New American Standard Bible (NASB), Copyright © 1960-1995 by
   The Lockman Foundation.
University of Chicago Press online, accessed June 23, 2011, http://
   www.press.uchicago.edu.
Faqs.org website, "Encyclopedia of Children and Childhood in
   History and Society: Polio," accessed July 5, 2014, http://
   www.faqs.org/childhood/Pa-Re/Polio.html.
University of Michigan School of Public Health website, "1955
   Polio Trial Vaccine Announcement," accessed July 5, 2014,
   https://sph.umich.edu/polio/.

Chapter Two

Saginaw News Courier, Friday, June 12, 1925, plosgene@sagi-
   nawlibrary.org.

Chapter Three

Revival Can Happen blog, accessed July 15, 2014, http://revival-
   canhappen.blogspot.com/2012/04/revival-quotes.html.

Chapter Four

Ohio History Central website, "The Great Depression," accessed
   July 5, 2010, http://www.ohiohistorycentral.org/w/Great_
   Depression?rec=500.
United Auto Workers Local 602 (Lansing, MI) website, "UAW:
   Sixty Years of Struggle," accessed July 5, 2010, www.lo-
   cal602.org.
Ehow, "Popular Dance Styles of 1930s," accessed August 4, 2013,
   www.ehow.com/list_7720397_dances-1920s-late-1930s.
   html#ixzz2b6r6vGmu.
Google, public domain photos Civilian Conservation Corps,
   accessed November 10, 2015, https:// www.google.com/

search?q=public+domain+photos+CCC+camps.

Google, public domain photos the Great Depression, accessed November 10, 2016, https://www.google.com/?gws_rd=ssl#q=public+domain+photos+great+depression.

Chapter Five

Harold Burnett, History of Bath Charter Township, 1826-1976 (Bath: Harold Burnett, 1978)

Wayfinding website, "Michigan Fever," accessed June 11, 2013, http://www.wayfinding.net/SS%20michigan%20fever.html.

Seeking Michigan website, accessed June 11, 2013, http://www.seekingmichigan.org/wp-content/uploads/2013/05/mitten_pioneer-life.pdf

The Michigan Historical Markers Website, "Chief Okemos/Okemos Village," accessed June 14, 2013, www.michmarkers.com/pages/12133.htm.

Library of Michigan, accessed June 14, 2013, www.michigan.gov/libraryofmichigan.

Michigan in Brief website, "About Michigan: Economic, Cultural and Political History," accessed June 14 and 16, 2013, http://www.michiganinbrief.org/edition07/Chapter1/Chapter1.htm.

Journey to the Past blog, "Pure Michigan Genealogy," accessed June 16, 2013, http://www.journeytothepastblog.com/2013/05/pure-michigan-genealogy-migration-and.html.

Breaking Through the Brick Walls (Cushman genealogy website), accessed July 2, 2013, http://www.cushmansite.com.

Christianity.com, "Layman Robert Cushman's Famous Sermon," accessed July 2, 2013, http://www.christianity.com/church/church-history/timeline/1601-1700/layman-robert-cushmans-famous-sermon-11630077.html.

Bliss Family in America, "Beyond Massachusetts, Rhode Island, and Connecticut," accessed July 5, 2013, www.usgennet.org/family/bliss/states/migrate.htm.

Ancestry.com, "Migration Patterns Message Boards," accessed July 5, 2013, www.ancestry.com Topics › Migration › Migration patterns Boards.Ancestry.com.

Scholastic Stacks, "Women's Rights Movement," accessed July 5, 2013, www.scholastic.com/browse/article.jsp?id=3753790.

Chapter Six

The Van Voorhees Association, "History of the Van Voorhees Family," accessed July 15, 2013, http://www.vanvoorhees. org/history.php.

The Van Voorhees Family in America: The First Six Generations (Gateway Press, Baltimore, MD).

The Van Voorhees Association Facebook page, "Origins of the Van Voorhees Before Coming to America, 1180-1660," accessed August 12, 2013, https://www.facebook.com/notes/ van-voorhees-association/origins-of-the-van-voorhees-be-fore-coming-to-america-1180-1660/155856124471430.

Jewish History website, accessed August 12, 2013, http://www. jewishhistory.org/.

Chapter Seven

M. J. Ellsworth, The Bath School Disaster (Bath, MI: M. J. Ellsworth, [1927] 2001), 75.

Grant Parker, Mayday: The History of a Village Holocaust (Perry, MI: Parker Press, 1980), 196-197.

Arnie Bernstein, Bath Massacre (University of Michigan Press, 2009), 13.

Google, "Public domain photos Bath School Disaster," accessed November 10, 2015, https://www.google.com/search?q=-public+domain+photos+Bath+School+Disaster&source=l-nms&tbm=isch&sa=X&ved=0ahUKEwjVtbKcq_rLAhXET-CYKHXqwCTMQ_AUIBygB&biw=1366&bih=643.

Chapter Eight

Harold Burnett, History of Bath Charter Township, 1826-1976

(Bath: Harold Burnett, 1978), 161, 199.
M. J. Ellsworth, The Bath School Disaster (Bath, MI: M. J. Ellsworth, [1927] 2001), 34-39, 40, 44.

Grant Parker, Mayday: The History of a Village Holocaust (Perry,
MI: Parker Press, 1980), 10-12, 16-17, 84, 98-99, 101-102, 243.

Arnie Bernstein, Bath Massacre (University of Michigan Press,
2009), 37, 42-43.

Google, "Public domain photos Bath School Disaster," accessed
November 10, 2015, https://www.google.com/search?q=-
public+domain+photos+Bath+School+Disaster&source=l-
nms&tbm=isch&sa=X&ved=0ahUKEwjVtbKcq_rLAhXET-
CYKHXqwCTMQ_AUIBygB&biw=1366&bih=643.

Chapter Nine

Carlton Hollister's letter, June, 1997.

Chapter Ten

Ann Cipo Whitney interview, June 10, 2010.
Google, "Public domain photos Bath School Disaster," accessed
November 10, 2015, https://www.google.com/search?q=-
public+domain+photos+Bath+School+Disaster&source=l-
nms&tbm=isch&sa=X&ved=0ahUKEwjVtbKcq_rLAhXET-
CYKHXqwCTMQ_AUIBygB&biw=1366&bih=643.

Chapter Eleven

Ancestry.com community page, "The Bath School Disaster,"
accessed May 3, 2015, http://freepages.history.rootsweb.
ancestry.com/~bauerle/disaster.htm.
Highland Ghost Hunters, "Bath School Disaster: Memorial Park
and Cemetery," accessed May 3, 2015, http://www.hgh-
paranormal.com/Pages/BathSchoolhouseDisaster.aspx.
Dean Sweet, Jr. interview, August 8, 2015.
M. J. Ellsworth, The Bath School Disaster (Bath, MI: M. J. Ells-

worth, [1927] 2001), 53, 67-69, 78-79, 81, 99, 118, 121, 127.
Grant Parker, Mayday: The History of a Village Holocaust (Perry, MI: Parker Press, 1980), 107, 114, 154.

Chapter Twelve

Wikipedia, "World War II," accessed May 3, 2015, https:// en.wikipedia.org/wiki/World_War_II.

Learn NC, a website of UNC School of Education, "World War II on the Homefront: Rationing," accessed May 3, 2015, http://www.learnnc.org/lp/editions/ww2-rationing/5934.

Wikipedia, "Rationing in the United States," accessed May 6, 2015, https://en.wikipedia.org/wiki/Rationing_in_the_United_States.

History.com, "Hungry History: Food Rationing in Wartime America," accessed May 6, 2015, http://www.history.com/news/hungry-history/food-rationing-in-wartime-america.

Wikipedia, "Rosie the Riveter," accessed May 6, 2015, https:// en.wikipedia.org/wiki/RosietheRiveter.

Pantagraph, "Kids Gathered Milkweed Pods for WWII Effort," accessed May 9, 2015, http://www.pantagraph.com/news/kids-gathered-milkweed-pods-for-wwii-effort/article_5099b3d3-117e-52c6-8815-c6893b97ea30.html.

The National World War II Museum New Orleans, "A Closer Look at War Bonds," accessed May 9, 2015, www.nationalww2museum.org/learn/education/for-students/ww2-history/take-a-closer-look/war-bonds.html.

Treasury Direct, "The History of U.S. Savings Bonds," accessed May 10, 2015, www.treasurydirect.gov/timeline.htm.

Wikipedia, "War Savings Stamps of the United States," accessed May 10, 2015, https://en.wikipedia.org/wiki/War_savings_stamps_of_the_United_States.

Wikipedia, "Women in World War II," accessed May 15, 2015, https://en.wikipedia.org/wiki/Women_in_World_War_II.

Wikipedia, "Battle of Leyte," accessed May 18, 2015, https:// en.wikipedia.org/wiki/Battle_of_Leyte.

History.com, "This Day in History: MacArthur Leaves the Philippines," accessed May 25, 2015, http://www.history.com/

this-day-in-history/macarthur-leaves-the-philippines.

Hall Wynne, "Frank J. Force," accessed June 5, 2015, http://www. hallwynne.com/frank-j-force/.

NavSource, "Amphibious Photo Archive, USS LST-709," accessed June 14, 2015, www.navsource.org/archives/10/16/160709. htm.

PBS, "The War: The Philippines (Leyte Gulf)," accessed June 14, 2015, http://www.pbs.org/thewar/detail_5226.htm.

Google, "Public domain photos WWII," accessed November 10, 2015, https://www.google.com/search?q=public+do-main+photos+WWII.

Chapter Thirteen

Ralph TerBeek Interview, July – August, 2010.

Wikipedia, "Camp Claiborne," accessed July 10, 2010, https:// en.wikipedia.org/wiki/Camp_Claiborne.

The WWII 300th Combat Engineers, "History of the 300th Combat Engineers, 1943 to 1945," http://www.300thcombatengi-neersinwwii.com/belvoir.html.

Island Farm Prisoner of War Camp 198: Brigend, South Wales, "Life in the Camp," accessed August 3, 2010, http://www. islandfarm.fsnet.co.uk/.

Wikipedia, "Omaha Beach," accessed August 6, 2010, https:// en.wikipedia.org/wiki/Omaha_Beach.

PBS American Experience, "Battle of the Bulge," accessed August 6, 2010, http://www.pbs.org/wgbh/americanexperience/ films/bulge/.

Wikipedia, "Operation Downfall," accessed August 10, 2010, https://en.wikipedia.org/wiki/Operation_Downfall.

Wikipedia, "Atomic Bombings of Hiroshima and Nagasaki," accessed August 10, 2010, https://en.wikipedia.org/wiki/ Atomic_bombings_of_Hiroshima_and_Nagasaki.

Chapter Fourteen

Memories of World War II Veterans (Moline Christian Reformed Church. Sterling Publishing, Moline, Michigan, June 1999)

Chapter Fifteen

ThatPoster.org, "Captain Fuchida," accessed August 8, 2015, http://www.thatposter.org/fuchida.html.

Bible Believers, Mitsuo Fuchida "From Pearl Harbor to Calvary," accessed August 8, 2015, www.biblebelievers.com/fuchida1.html.

Stars and Stripes, "Pearl Harbor Pilot Became Evangelist," accessed August 9, 2015, www.stripes.com/news/pearl-harbor-pilot-became-evangelist-1.85934.

Wikipedia, "Mitsuo Fuchida," accessed August 9, 2015, https://en.wikipedia.org/wiki/Mitsuo_Fuchida.

ForDummies.com, "World War II Comes to America: Pearl Harbor," accessed August 9, 2015, http://www.dummies.com/how-to/content/world-war-ii-comes-to-america-pearl-harbor.html.

History.com, "Pearl Harbor," accessed August 12, 2015, http://www.history.com/topics/world-war-ii/pearl-harbor.

History.com, "Battle of Midway," accessed August 18, **2015,** http://www.history.com/topics/world-war-ii/battle-of-midway.

Google, "Public domain photos POW Jake DeShazer," accessed November 10, 2015, https://www.google.com/search?q=public+domain+photos+POW+Jake+DeShazer&source=lnms&tbm=isch&sa=X&ved=0ahUKEwj21Mzv8vrLAhXMLSYKHYoWCoQQ_AUIBygB&biw=1366&bih=643.

Made in the USA
Monee, IL
13 February 2022

90330851R00114